Buddy Oliver
LET'S COOK

Photography DAVID LOFTUS & PAUL STUART

MICHAEL  JOSEPH

CONTENTS

Breakfast toastie

Peasto pasta

Mini quiches

Rocky road

Barbecued chicken lollipops

Quick and easy pizzas

All-rounder tomato sauce

HELLO, IT'S BUDDY!

First of all, I want to say that I'm happy you're here! Cooking is one of my all-time favourite things to do. It's really fun, and a great skill to learn. Once you know the basics, you can give most recipes a try, or even have a go at making your own! It doesn't always go to plan, but that doesn't matter. I like to cook for my brother and sisters, but I also cook for my friends sometimes. If you make something – exactly how you like it – you'll want to eat it, and it's good not always having to rely on grown-ups!

One of the first things I ever cooked was scrambled eggs – they were really tasty, and actually so simple once you know how. It made me want to see what else I could do. I learnt to make things like chopped salads from helping Mum or Dad in the kitchen, and even started to make pizza and bread. The more I learnt, the more I wanted to explore.

This book is full of the things I love to cook and eat. It's not fancy or hard to do, it's just simple food done nicely (I hope you agree). My absolute favourite recipe is the Easy meatballs and spaghetti because it's fun to make and tastes so good. I'm a big pasta fan, so there's a whole chapter of easy pastas in the book.

My family favourites chapter is probably the one I cook from most. It's all the things I like to eat at home, and can now make myself – things like fajitas, fishcakes, Bolognese and fish finger sarnies. I've also got some tasty breakfast and brunch recipes – brunch is for when you've got a bit more time to enjoy eating at the weekend, and that's when I tend to have more time to cook, too. I've included some after-school bites – things you can eat quickly when you get home. I'm always hungry then! And I also love to make cakes and puds because they're sweet and delicious, but I do sometimes make a bit of a mess!

I've had so much fun in the last few years creating *Cooking Buddies* and sharing my recipes. Making the TV show was epic – it was really fun to learn some cool new skills from other kids, but also to teach them dishes that they can share with their friends. You can watch all of the *Cooking Buddies* episodes on BBC iPlayer, plus there's lots more great how-to and recipe videos on my *Cooking Buddies* YouTube channel. Have fun!

A WORD FROM DAD

There's something so powerful about being able to cook. You could even call it a superpower – one that grants you real freedom when it comes to what you want to eat. I'll let you in on a little secret: the key to learning to cook is being curious and having the confidence to give it a go. Not everything will work out perfectly – and that's OK. Sometimes, when things don't go to plan, you might still end up with something delicious, just not what you were expecting!

Buddy and his brother and sisters have all grown up around food, but Buddy, out of all of them, has always found it effortlessly exciting – a real adventure. He's been my shadow in the kitchen since he was tiny, and the skills he's clocked up are unreal. I'm super-proud of this book and the effort he's put into building up *Cooking Buddies* over the last few years.

Now, even if this is your first cookbook, you're never too young to start making incredible things, getting stuck in, having a laugh and enjoying yourself along the way. Think of a recipe a bit like a treasure trail – something that gets you from A to B – with a prize (a tasty bite to eat!) at the end. It really is super-fun. I was just eight years old when I properly started to cook, and I haven't looked back since.

So, guys, what are you waiting for? Put coloured stickies on the pages of the things you want to try, and ask a grown-up if you can get the ingredients and give them a go. Get those adults working for you ;)

NOW GROWN-UPS...

Please believe me when I say, you will never regret encouraging your children to learn how to cook. I'm not talking about cheffy recipes with complicated techniques, just good, simple, nutritious, fun food that will help fuel your kids with the right stuff. Trust me, knowing how to make a bowl of pasta or a simple soup are skills that will set them up for life.

There's something incredibly powerful about giving kids the freedom to make their own decisions about the food they eat. Having a bit of control over the shopping and the cooking means that they can make it in the way they like it, which will ultimately help us out on our quest to get them eating well. Lots of parents are lost when it comes to the quirks of feeding their kids (me included!), so it's always worth trying a new approach.

Knowing how to cook is one of the most important gifts you can give a child, and if you want to brush up on your own kitchen skills, too, why not pick a new recipe and make it together. It's wonderful to see the sense of pride when a child realizes that they can make a valuable contribution to family mealtimes.

On the pages that follow, you'll find a lovely bunch of tested and trusted recipes for you and your family to use week in, week out. There's a mixture of cool and contemporary dishes, a whole collection of family favourites (with plenty of the good stuff built in!), as well as after-school bites and some much-loved sweet treats. Buddy has also included a chapter called 'Skills for life', which is full of basic recipes you can work your way through to really tick off those easy, but important, everyday kitchen skills. And remember, don't worry if you don't have the exact ingredients listed on each page, you can be flexible with the type or variety, or swap things in and out as you please – for things like oil, cheese or seasonal produce, choose your favourite or just use what you have to hand.

I hope that this book will help your kids to fall in love with a whole rainbow of beautiful ingredients and flavours.

Big love, Jamie O xxx

BREAKFAST AND BRUNCH

Breakfast toastie

With a baked bean dipper

You need

20g Cheddar cheese

2 slices of bread

1 large egg

optional: 2 rashers of smoked
streaky bacon

100g baked beans or homemade
beans (see page 122)

1   Switch your toastie maker on to warm up.

2   Grate the cheese over one of the slices of bread.

3   Push and squash the bread down to create a pocket in the centre, then
carefully crack in the egg and top with the second piece of bread.

4   Stretch out the bacon rashers slightly, then carefully wrap them around
the outside of the bread (if using).

5   Carefully transfer to the toastie maker, then clamp the lid down and
toast for 5 minutes, or until golden and crisp.

6   Warm the beans through in a small pan or in the microwave, and
serve alongside.

66 If using regular baked beans
here, spice them up with a shake of
Worcestershire sauce and a dash or
two of Tabasco – so good! 99

Egg tortilla wrap

With salsa and smashed avo

You need

85g wholemeal flour

olive oil

1 large ripe tomato (150g)

3 spring onions

1 small red pepper

½ a bunch of basil (15g)

red wine vinegar

½ a ripe avocado

4 medium eggs

20g Cheddar cheese

Time-saver alert!

Swap in shop-bought tortillas to speed this one right up!

1   Tip the flour into a mixing bowl, add a pinch of sea salt, then make a well in the middle. Pour in 50ml of warm water and 1 tablespoon of olive oil, then use a fork to bring in the flour from the outside to form a dough – when the dough starts to come together, dust your hands with flour and pat it into a ball.

2   Knead on a flour-dusted surface for a few minutes, or until smooth and elastic. Leave to rest for 30 minutes.

3   Deseed the tomato and roughly chop three-quarters of it, trim and finely slice 2 spring onions and deseed and finely chop the pepper, then scrape into a bowl. Tear in the basil leaves, drizzle with 1 teaspoon each of olive oil and red wine vinegar, then toss together and season to taste.

4   Peel and destone the avocado (if needed), scoop into a bowl, then mash with a fork. Trim the remaining spring onion and finely dice with the leftover tomato, then stir into the avocado.

5   Split the dough in half, roll each piece into a ball, then use a rolling pin to roll each one out into a circle, roughly 24cm in diameter.

6   Put a 24cm non-stick frying pan on a medium heat and, one at a time, cook the tortillas for 1 minute on each side, then remove.

7   Beat the eggs in a jug with a pinch of salt and black pepper.

8   Drizzle 1 teaspoon of olive oil into the pan, then carefully wipe it round with a ball of kitchen paper. Pour in half the egg, tilt the pan to coat, place a cooked tortilla on top and cook for 1 minute, then flip.

9   Finely grate over half the cheese, leave for 30 seconds to 1 minute to melt, then slide carefully on to a plate.

10   Spread half the smashed avo on to the tortilla, scatter over half the tomato salsa, then roll up. Repeat with the rest of the ingredients.

Chocolatey porridge

With yoghurt and fresh fruit

You need

200g blanched almonds

100g Medjool dates

400g porridge oats

2 teaspoons ground cinnamon

3 heaped tablespoons quality
    cocoa powder

1 orange

To serve (per portion)

200ml milk

1 heaped tablespoon
    Greek or natural yoghurt

80g fresh fruit, such as orange
    segments, blueberries,
    raspberries, blackberries, sliced
    banana, grated apple and pear

1   Tip the almonds into a dry non-stick frying pan on a medium heat and toast until golden, stirring regularly, then tip into a food processor.

2   Remove the stones from the dates, then tear the flesh into the processor. Add half the oats, the cinnamon and the cocoa powder.

3   Finely grate in the orange zest and pulse until fine, then stir the mixture back through the rest of the oats. Tip into an airtight jar, ready to use – it'll keep for a couple of weeks (or more!).

4   To make a bowl of porridge, simply put 65g of the mixture into a saucepan with 200ml of milk (per portion) and heat over a medium-low heat for 3 minutes, or until it's the consistency that you like, stirring regularly and adding splashes of water to loosen, if needed.

5   Top each bowlful with a spoonful of Greek yoghurt and your favourite seasonal fruit. Just remember, if you cook multiple portions at once, simply adjust the cooking time slightly.

Did you know?

Using great-quality cocoa powder here instead of regular chocolate will give you that much-loved chocolatey goodness, but it's nutritious for you, too – bonus!

Rainbow smoothies

With banana, milk and almonds or oats

You need

1 banana

3 tablespoons ground almonds
or 25g porridge oats

250ml milk

2 handfuls of frozen mango, frozen
mixed berries, frozen cherries or
baby spinach (or a mixture)

1 Peel and slice the banana (ideally you want to use a frozen banana,
so try to remember to do this the day before).

2 Put the banana, ground almonds or oats and milk into a blender. Add
your chosen flavour combo, secure the lid and blitz until smooth.

3 Pour into glasses, then serve.

Over-ripe bananas?

Peel and roughly chop any bananas that are on the turn, squeeze
over a little lime juice (this stops the bananas going brown), then
pop them into a reusable freezer bag in a single layer, to stop them
sticking together, and freeze until solid.

Poached eggs

You need

2 large eggs

1 English muffin

unsalted butter

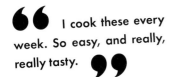

I cook these every week. So easy, and really, really tasty.

1 Half-fill a large pan with boiling water, add a pinch of sea salt, then bring to a light simmer over a medium heat.

2 Crack one of the eggs into a cup, then gently pour it into the water in one go, and repeat – the eggs will start to cook straight away, and don't worry if the edges look a bit wispy.

3 For a really soft poached egg, cook for around 2 minutes, and for a soft-to-firm egg, cook for 4 minutes – these times might vary slightly depending on the pan you use.

4 To check whether the eggs are done, lift one out of the water with a slotted spoon and give it a gentle poke with a teaspoon. If it feels too soft, carefully pop it back for an extra minute or two. When you're happy, remove the eggs to kitchen paper to dry off.

5 Halve the muffin and toast until golden, then spread lightly with butter and spoon a poached egg on to each half.

Scrambled eggs

You need

2 eggs

optional: 1 sprig of soft herbs, such as flat-leaf parsley, chives

unsalted butter

1 slice of bread

1 Crack the eggs into a jug, season with a pinch of sea salt and black pepper, and beat together well.

2 Pick, finely chop and add the herbs (if using). Place a knob of butter in a non-stick pan on a low heat, and once melted, pour in the eggs.

3 Stir slowly with a spatula until the eggs look silky and slightly underdone, then remove from the heat.

4 Toast and butter the bread, then place on a serving plate and spoon over the scrambled eggs.

Fried eggs

You need

olive oil

2 eggs

1 slice of bread

unsalted butter

1 Drizzle 2 tablespoons of olive oil into a large non-stick frying pan on a medium-low heat.

2 Carefully crack the eggs into the pan, and when they turn white, tilt the pan and carefully spoon some of the hot oil over the eggs – this will help them to cook through evenly.

3 Use a fish slice to carefully transfer the eggs to kitchen paper to drain, gently patting them dry.

4 Toast and butter the bread, place on a serving plate and spoon over the fried eggs.

Boiled eggs

You need

2 large eggs

1 slice of bread

unsalted butter

1 Place a small saucepan of boiling salted water on a high heat and bring to a fast boil.

2 Using a tablespoon, dip the eggs in and out of the water a few times (this helps to stop them cracking through shock), then slowly lower them into the pan.

3 Cook for the following times, depending on how you like your eggs: 5 minutes for runny or 7½ minutes for semi-firm (if you want to make a hard-boiled egg, cook for 10 minutes), then remove to an egg cup.

4 Toast and butter the bread, then cut into soldiers. Lightly tap and remove the top of the egg and start dunking.

Savoury breakfast muffins

With a crunchy seed topping

You need

80g Cheddar or Parmesan cheese

125g baby spinach

optional: 1 red chilli

2 spring onions

200ml milk

50ml olive oil

2 large eggs

350g wholemeal self-raising flour

50g feta cheese

2 tablespoons mixed seeds, such as sesame, sunflower, pumpkin, poppy

1   Preheat the oven to 180°C, and line a muffin tin with 12 paper cases.

2   Grate the Cheddar or Parmesan and place in a mixing bowl. Finely chop half the spinach and roughly chop the rest, then add to the bowl.

3   Deseed and finely chop the chilli (if using), trim and finely chop the spring onions, then add to the bowl.

4   Pour the milk and olive oil into a separate mixing bowl, crack in the eggs and mix well. Fold through the flour, a pinch of sea salt and all the ingredients from the other bowl.

5   Spoon half the mixture between the 12 paper cases, crumble the feta and divide between them, then spoon over the rest of the mixture. Sprinkle over your chosen seeds, then bake for 20 minutes, or until golden and cooked through – if you poke a skewer into the middle, it should come out clean.

6   Allow to cool slightly in the tin, then transfer to a wire cooling rack – delicious served warm or cold.

Bonus flavour

If you've got any leftover ham, roast chicken or different cheeses, or even things like olives and tomatoes, these can all be chopped up and added to this recipe – it's super-flexible!

Eggy bread

With raspberry ripple yoghurt and nut butter

You need

2 large eggs

2 tablespoons milk

2 x 1.5cm slices of bread

olive oil

2 teaspoons your favourite
nut butter

160g raspberries

2 heaped tablespoons
natural yoghurt

optional: 1 sprig of mint

runny honey, to serve

1 Crack the eggs into a shallow bowl, add the milk, then whisk together.

2 Place a large non-stick frying pan on a medium heat to heat up.

3 Add the bread to the bowl and gently squash to soak up the egg mixture (a bit like a sponge!), turning a few times.

4 Drizzle ½ a tablespoon of olive oil into the frying pan and carefully swirl the pan around to evenly coat the inside.

5 One at a time, lift the soaked bread up in the bowl and allow the excess mixture to drip off, then carefully place in the pan. Cook for 2 to 3 minutes on each side, or until golden and cooked through, then transfer to serving plates and spread with the nut butter.

6 Roughly mash half the raspberries with the yoghurt, then divide between plates, scattering over the rest of the berries.

7 Pick, chop and scatter over the mint leaves (if using) and drizzle lightly with honey, to finish.

Bonus flavour

Adding a good pinch of ground cinnamon to the egg mixture before you cook it will take the flavour to the next level. Give it a try!

FAMILY FAVOURITES

Quick and easy pizzas

With your favourite topping combo

You need

2 cloves of garlic

olive oil

1 x 400g tin of plum tomatoes

400g self-raising flour,
    plus extra for dusting

80g mozzarella cheese

optional: 4 chipolata sausages

4 handfuls of your favourite
    vegetables, such as peppers,
    cherry tomatoes, sweetcorn,
    broccoli, onion, black olives

time-saver alert!

If you have any all-rounder tomato sauce (see page 132) left over, feel free to swap it in here to save yourself time.

1   Peel and finely slice the garlic, then place in a pan on a medium heat with 1 tablespoon of olive oil and fry until golden.

2   Scrunch in the tomatoes (or tip in and break up with a spoon as you go), simmer for 5 minutes, or until thickened slightly, then season to taste with sea salt and black pepper. Remove from the heat.

3   Preheat the oven to 220°C and rub the inside of a 25cm x 35cm baking tray with olive oil.

4   Tip the flour into a mixing bowl, add a pinch of salt, then make a well in the middle. Pour in 250ml of water, then use a fork to stir and bring in the flour from the outside to form a dough – when the dough starts to come together, dust your hands with flour and pat it into a ball.

5   Knead on a flour-dusted surface for a few minutes, or until smooth and elastic. Divide the dough into 4, then roll and stretch the pieces into 20cm rounds or ovals.

6   Spread each base generously with the tomato sauce and tear over the mozzarella. Squeeze the sausagemeat (if using) out of the skins and tear over the pizzas, then prep and scatter over your chosen vegetable toppings.

7   Drizzle lightly with olive oil, then cook on the top shelf of the oven for 10 minutes, or until golden and puffed up. Delicious served with a crunchy green salad.

" You can swap in veg oil for olive oil, if that's what you've got, and Cheddar or red Leicester for mozzarella. "

Chicken fajitas

With zingy corn salsa

You need

1 large red onion

1 large red pepper

2 x 150g skinless chicken breasts

1 teaspoon sweet smoked paprika

½ teaspoon ground cumin

olive oil

1 corn on the cob

2 spring onions

½ a red chilli

½ a bunch of coriander (15g)

1 lime

8 small wholemeal flour tortillas

1 baby gem or ¼ of an iceberg lettuce

60g Cheddar cheese

75g natural yoghurt

1 Peel and finely slice the onion, deseed and finely slice the pepper and finely slice the chicken, then transfer it all to a large mixing bowl.

2 Add the paprika, cumin, 1 teaspoon of olive oil and a pinch of sea salt and black pepper, then toss together.

3 To make the corn salsa, char the corn in a dry non-stick frying pan over a high heat for 8 minutes, turning regularly. Leave to cool, then carefully slice the kernels off the husk.

4 Place the corn kernels in a bowl, then finely chop and add the spring onions, chilli and 1 sprig of coriander. Squeeze over half the lime juice, mix well and season with a little pepper. Slice the leftover lime half into wedges, to serve.

5 Warm the tortillas in the microwave (keep warm until needed), shred the lettuce, grate the cheese and pick the leftover coriander leaves.

6 Place a large non-stick frying pan on a high heat, then tip in the chicken and vegetables and cook for 5 minutes, or until the chicken is golden and cooked through, stirring regularly.

7 Carefully take the pan of sizzling chicken and vegetables to the table (pop a protective mat underneath!) with the tortillas, corn salsa, lettuce, grated cheese, coriander leaves, yoghurt and lime wedges, and get everyone to load up their own fajitas.

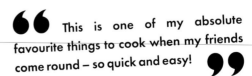

66 This is one of my absolute favourite things to cook when my friends come round – so quick and easy! 99

The ultimate burger

With melty cheese and salad

You need

4 gherkins

2 ripe tomatoes

200g red cabbage

red wine vinegar

½ an iceberg lettuce

½ a cucumber

extra virgin olive oil

1 x 400g tin of green lentils

250g minced beef
   or veggie mince

olive oil

4 slices of Cheddar cheese
   (60g total)

4 small burger buns

optional: tomato ketchup
   and/or mayo

1   Slice the gherkins (use a crinkle-cut knife, if you've got one) and tomatoes, and set aside. Finely slice or grate the red cabbage, then toss in a mixing bowl with 1 tablespoon of red wine vinegar.

2   Shred the lettuce and slice the cucumber, then place in another mixing bowl and dress with 1 tablespoon of extra virgin olive oil.

3   Drain the lentils and pat dry with kitchen paper, then blitz in a food processor with the mince and a pinch of black pepper. Divide the mixture into 4 equal pieces and shape into 3cm-thick patties.

4   Place a large non-stick frying pan on a medium heat. Brush the patties with 1 tablespoon of olive oil, then carefully place in the hot pan and cook for 4 minutes on each side, or until just cooked through, nudging the patties towards the edge of the pan to sear the sides.

5   When the burgers are looking good, place a slice of cheese on top of each one, add a splash of water to the pan (the steam will help the cheese to melt), then cover for an extra minute, or until melted.

6   Cut the buns in half (toast them if you like), add a dollop of ketchup and/or mayo (if using) to each base, then place a burger on top.

7   Layer the gherkin, tomato and cucumber slices, and a pinch of lettuce on top of each one, then pop the lids on. Serve the rest of the lettuce, cucumber and tomato on the side, along with the pickled cabbage.

66 Homemade burgers are fast, fun and taste juicier than the ones you buy. Plus, you can stack up the toppings and layer in your favourite sauces exactly as you like them. **99**

Tasty tomato soup

With melty cheese dunkers

You need

1 carrot

1 onion

1 clove of garlic

1 celery stick

olive oil

1 vegetable or chicken stock cube

2 x 400g tins of plum tomatoes

4 slices of bread

85g Cheddar cheese

a few sprigs of basil

200ml milk

1 tablespoon balsamic vinegar

1 Peel and chop the carrot, onion and garlic, then trim and finely slice the celery. Place a large saucepan on a medium heat, drizzle in 1 tablespoon of olive oil, then scrape in the chopped vegetables.

2 Cook for 10 minutes with the lid on (leaving a little gap), or until softened, stirring occasionally. Crumble in the stock cube, carefully top up with 500ml of boiling water and stir to dissolve.

3 Scrunch in the tomatoes (or tip in and break up with a spoon as you go), then turn the heat up to high and bring to the boil. Reduce the heat to low, pop the lid back on and simmer for 10 minutes, or until thickened slightly, stirring occasionally.

4 Toast one side of the bread slices under the grill until golden, turn over, then coarsely grate over the Cheddar and place back under the grill until oozy and melty.

5 Remove the pan from the heat, pick in most of the basil leaves and pour in the milk and balsamic, then carefully blitz with a stick blender until smooth (use a tea towel to protect your hands from little splashes).

6 Taste and season, if needed, then ladle the soup into serving bowls or mugs. Slice the toast into soldiers and serve on the side for dunking.

Time-saver alert!

Although prepping vegetables is a great way to practise your knife skills, if you want to save time, swap the carrot, onion and celery for 300g of ready-prepped frozen diced base veg mix – you can find this in most supermarkets.

Barbecue ribs

With a sticky-sweet glaze

You need

optional: 1 fresh red chilli

3cm piece of ginger

2 cloves of garlic

150ml unsweetened apple juice

100ml white wine vinegar

2 tablespoons tomato ketchup

1 tablespoon Dijon mustard

2 tablespoons low-salt soy sauce

100g runny honey

olive oil

2 racks of pork loin back ribs
(roughly 1.6kg)

1   Preheat the oven to 200°C. Deseed and finely chop the chilli (if using), peel and grate the ginger and garlic, then place it all in a medium pan. Add the apple juice, vinegar, ketchup, mustard, soy and honey, and whisk together. Cook over a medium heat for 10 minutes, or until thickened slightly.

2   Drizzle a little olive oil over the ribs, season with black pepper and rub all over to coat, then place in a large roasting tray lined with a double layer of tin foil.

3   Brush the ribs generously with the marinade, then cover the tray tightly with foil. Roast for 30 minutes, then remove the tray from the oven, take off the foil, and baste with the marinade. Preheat your barbecue at this stage (if using).

4   Carefully put the foil back on and return the ribs to the oven for a further 30 minutes, or until the meat pulls easily away from the bone.

5   Remove the tray from the oven and discard the foil, baste again, then either return to the oven, uncovered, for 15 minutes, or transfer to the barbecue over a medium-low heat for 5 to 10 minutes, or until beautifully sticky and caramelized.

6   Transfer the ribs to a board, slice up and serve. Delicious with a crunchy green salad and new potatoes.

Easy fishcakes

With Cheddar, lemon and parsley

You need

600g potatoes

olive oil

2 x 120g salmon fillets, skin off, pin-boned

a few sprigs of flat-leaf parsley

1 lemon

50g Cheddar cheese

25g plain flour

1 Peel the potatoes, chop into 3cm chunks and cook in a pan of boiling salted water for 12 minutes, or until tender.

2 Drizzle 1 tablespoon of olive oil into a large non-stick frying pan on a medium heat, add the salmon and cook for 6 to 8 minutes, or until just cooked through, turning regularly, then leave to cool.

3 Pick and finely chop the parsley, finely grate the lemon zest and coarsely grate the Cheddar.

4 Drain the potatoes and leave to steam dry for a few minutes, then tip back into the pan and mash with a potato masher.

5 Scrape in the parsley, lemon zest and Cheddar, season with a pinch of sea salt and black pepper, then mix together. Flake in the salmon and fold through, shape into 4 patties, then coat all over in the flour.

6 Place the frying pan back on a medium heat and cook the fishcakes for 3 minutes on each side, or until beautifully golden.

7 Cut the lemon into wedges for squeezing over. Delicious served with a green salad or peas.

Flavour switch-up

You can take this basic recipe in lots of different directions by simply adding or swapping in one or two ingredients. Why not try adding a little curry paste or some fresh chilli for a bit of a kick, or change up the herbs (basil, mint, coriander or chives are delicious). You can use tinned fish in place of the fresh salmon, if you prefer, and a handful of cooked chopped prawns thrown into the mix are really yummy, too.

Crispy chicken

With slaw, corn and wedges

You need

1–2 thick slices of wholemeal
bread (roughly 80g)

½ a clove of garlic

2 x 120g skinless chicken breasts

400g Maris Piper potatoes

olive oil

2 corn on the cobs

½ a red onion

1 small carrot

½ an eating apple

200g white cabbage

½ teaspoon English mustard

½ tablespoon extra virgin olive oil

1 tablespoon white wine vinegar

2 heaped tablespoons
natural yoghurt

1 Preheat the oven to 200°C. Tear the bread into a food processor, peel and add the garlic, then whiz until fine.

2 Place the chicken breasts between two sheets of greaseproof paper, then use a rolling pin or the base of a heavy pan to bash and flatten them out to around 1cm thick.

3 Lift up the bashed chicken breasts, pour half the breadcrumbs on to the paper, put the chicken back on top, and scatter over the rest of the crumbs. Roughly pat the breadcrumbs on to the chicken, then re-cover with the paper and bash again to help them stick.

4 Scrub the potatoes, then slice into wedges (use a crinkle-cut knife, if you've got one) and place in a large mixing bowl. Season with a pinch of sea salt and black pepper and drizzle in 1 tablespoon of olive oil, then toss together to coat.

5 Spread out in a single layer on a large baking tray and bake for 35 minutes, or until golden and cooked through, giving the tray a shake and adding the corn to the oven for the last 10 minutes.

6 Peel the onion and coarsely grate on a box grater or in a food processor (or slice by hand) with the carrot, apple (discarding the core) and cabbage. Tip into a mixing bowl, mix with the mustard, extra virgin olive oil, vinegar and yoghurt, then season to taste.

7 When the wedges have 10 minutes to go, place a large non-stick frying pan on a medium heat with 1 tablespoon of olive oil and fry the chicken for 3 minutes on each side, or until golden and cooked through, adding an extra drizzle of oil, if needed.

8 Remove the chicken to a board, slice 1cm thick, and serve with the wedges, corn and slaw. Delicious with tomato ketchup for dipping.

Buddy's Bolognese

With sausages, minced beef and grated vegetables

You need

2 pork sausages

olive oil

500g lean minced beef

2 onions

2 cloves of garlic

1 large carrot

1 celery stick

1 courgette

2 tablespoons thick
   balsamic vinegar

2 x 400g tins of plum tomatoes

1 heaped teaspoon tomato purée

450g your favourite dried pasta

Parmesan cheese, to serve

1   Place a large casserole pan on a medium-high heat to warm up.

2   Squeeze the sausagemeat out of the skins.

3   Drizzle 1 tablespoon of olive oil into the pan, add the minced beef and sausagemeat, breaking everything up with a spoon as you go, then cook for 5 minutes, stirring regularly.

4   Peel the onions and garlic, trim the carrot, celery and courgette, then coarsely grate all the vegetables on a box grater, finely grating the garlic. Scrape into the pan, then reduce the heat to medium-low and cook for 10 minutes, or until soft and sweet, stirring occasionally.

5   Add the balsamic vinegar, then scrunch in the tomatoes (or tip in and break up with a spoon as you go). Half-fill each tin with water, swirl around to pick up the last bits of tomato and pour it into the pan.

6   Stir in the tomato purée and a pinch of black pepper, mash everything up with the spoon, then reduce the heat to low and leave to cook for 1 hour, or until thickened slightly.

7   About 15 minutes before you're ready to serve, cook the pasta in a large pan of boiling salted water according to the packet instructions, then drain, reserving a mugful of starchy cooking water.

8   Carefully add the pasta to the sauce and stir well over the heat, loosening with a splash of pasta water, if needed. Divide between serving bowls, and finish with a good grating of Parmesan.

Green pancake stack

Creamy spinach sauce, cheese and ham

You need

2 large eggs

175g plain flour

850ml milk

175g baby spinach

50g unsalted butter

2 cloves of garlic

olive oil

150g Cheddar cheese

optional: 100g smoked ham

1 butterhead or round lettuce

red wine vinegar

Easy swaps

Dress the salad with whatever vinegar and oil you have in the cupboard.

1 Preheat the oven to 180°C. For the pancakes, crack the eggs into a blender, add 125g of flour, 150ml of milk, 25g of spinach and a pinch of sea salt and black pepper, then blitz until smooth.

2 Put a saucepan on a medium heat with the butter, then peel, finely slice and add the garlic and cook for 2 minutes, or until softened.

3 Stir in 50g of flour and gradually pour in 700ml of milk, then cook until thickened slightly. Stir in the leftover spinach and season to taste.

4 Put a 26cm non-stick frying pan on a medium heat with 1 tablespoon of olive oil. Add just enough batter to coat the base of the pan, gently swirling it to cover, cook until lightly golden, then flip and cook on the other side. Repeat with the remaining batter, wiping out the pan with a ball of kitchen paper and adding a tiny drizzle of oil each time – you should end up with 5 thin pancakes.

5 Meanwhile, grate the cheese and tear up the ham (if using).

6 If your frying pan isn't ovenproof, get yourself a deep ovenproof pan or dish (26cm in diameter). Repeat the layers of pancake, spinach sauce, ham and cheese until you've used up all the ingredients, finishing with a layer of sauce and cheese.

7 Bake for 30 minutes, or until golden and bubbling, then rest for 10 minutes before serving.

8 Click apart the lettuce leaves, toss with 3 tablespoons of olive oil and 1 tablespoon of red wine vinegar, then season to taste and serve alongside the pancake stack.

Sausage and bean casserole

With peppers and gentle spices

You need

6 pork or veggie sausages

2 red onions

2 cloves of garlic

2 celery sticks

2 red peppers

olive oil

2 teaspoons sweet
  smoked paprika

1 teaspoon ground cumin

1 tablespoon brown sauce

2 x 400g tins of plum tomatoes

2 x 400g tins of cannellini beans

optional: a few sprigs of
  flat-leaf parsley

1   Preheat the grill to medium. Prick the sausages, then grill for 10 minutes, or until browned all over, turning halfway. Remove to kitchen paper to drain, patting them dry.

2   Peel the onions and garlic, trim the celery and deseed the peppers, then roughly chop. Drizzle 1 tablespoon of olive oil into a large non-stick casserole pan on a medium heat, add the chopped vegetables, then cook for 10 minutes, or until softened, stirring regularly.

3   Add the paprika, cumin and brown sauce, and cook for a further 2 minutes. Scrunch in the tomatoes (or tip in and break up with a spoon as you go). Fill the tin with water, swirl it around to pick up the last bits of tomato and pour it into the pan.

4   Add the beans (juices and all), stir well, then bring to the boil, while you slice up the sausages and add them to the pan.

5   Turn the heat down to low and cook for 40 minutes, or until thickened slightly, adding splashes of water to loosen, if needed. Taste and season with sea salt and black pepper, if needed, then pick and tear over the parsley (if using). Tasty served with green veggies and perfect rice (see page 138), mashed potato or baked potatoes (see page 142).

66 If I've got any stale bread hanging around, I sometimes whiz it into fine breadcrumbs, toast until golden and sprinkle over the top before tucking in. 99

Fish finger sarnies

With sweet potato chips

You need

4 sweet potatoes (800g total)

1 teaspoon smoked paprika

olive oil

25g plain flour

1 large egg

1–2 thick slices of wholemeal
  bread (roughly 80g)

optional: 15g Cheddar or
  Parmesan cheese

4 x 120g white fish or salmon
  fillets, skin off, pin-boned

2 tablespoons tomato ketchup

4 heaped tablespoons natural
  yoghurt

1 little gem lettuce

4 submarine rolls

1 Preheat the oven to 200°C. Scrub the sweet potatoes clean, slice each one into chunky chips (use a crinkle-cut knife, if you've got one), then tip them on to a large baking tray.

2 Season lightly with sea salt, black pepper and the smoked paprika, then drizzle over 1 tablespoon of olive oil and toss to coat. Spread out in a single layer on the tray and bake for 35 minutes, or until golden and cooked through.

3 Sprinkle the flour on to a plate and beat the egg in a shallow bowl. Whiz the bread in a food processor with the cheese (if using), 2 tablespoons of olive oil and a pinch of salt and pepper until fine, then tip on to a baking tray. Line a second tray with greaseproof paper.

4 Carefully slice each fish fillet in half lengthways (it doesn't matter if they're slightly different shapes). Turn each one in the flour until evenly coated, dip into the egg, letting any excess drip off, then turn in the breadcrumbs until well coated all over.

5 Transfer to the lined tray (at this stage you can freeze the fish fingers, so feel free to double up and have some extras for another day).

6 When the chips have 15 minutes to go, add the tray of fish fingers to the oven until golden and cooked through (cook them for 20 minutes if cooking straight from frozen).

7 Mix the ketchup and yoghurt together to make a kinda Marie Rose sauce, trim and finely shred the lettuce, and slice the rolls in half.

8 Load up the bases of the rolls with a spoonful of the sauce and a handful of shredded lettuce, then place 2 fish fingers on each one, and pop the lids on. Serve the sweet potato chips alongside.

Vegetable curry

With cooling cucumber yoghurt

You need

600g butternut squash

2 tablespoons curry powder

½ a bunch of coriander (15g)

2 onions

2 cloves of garlic

3cm piece of ginger

250g cauliflower

4 ripe tomatoes

olive oil

1 vegetable stock cube

1 x 400g tin of light coconut milk

1 x 400g tin of chickpeas

½ a cucumber

½ a bunch of mint (15g)

150g natural yoghurt

1 lemon

100g baby spinach

1 Peel and deseed the squash, chop into 2cm chunks, then toss in a mixing bowl with 1 tablespoon of curry powder and a pinch of sea salt and black pepper.

2 Pick the coriander leaves and finely chop the stalks. Peel and finely slice the onions, then peel and finely chop the garlic and ginger. Slice the cauliflower into florets, thinly slicing any stalk, and roughly chop the tomatoes.

3 Drizzle 1 tablespoon of olive oil into a large non-stick pan on a medium heat, add the squash and cook for 6 minutes, or until softened, stirring occasionally, then remove to a plate.

4 Place the pan back on a medium heat with 1 tablespoon of olive oil, the coriander stalks, 1 tablespoon of curry powder, and the onion, garlic and ginger. Cook for 5 minutes, stirring occasionally.

5 Crumble in the stock cube, then pour in 150ml of boiling water along with the coconut milk. Add the tomatoes, squash and chickpeas (juices and all), then cook over a low heat for 30 minutes, or until thickened slightly, adding the cauliflower for the last 10 minutes.

6 To make the cucumber yoghurt, halve the cucumber lengthways and scrape out the seeds, then coarsely grate into a bowl. Pick, finely chop and add the mint leaves, then stir in the yoghurt and a squeeze of lemon juice. Taste and season, if needed.

7 When the time's up on the curry, stir in the spinach and allow to wilt, then taste and adjust the seasoning, if needed.

8 Scatter over the coriander leaves, and serve with the cucumber yoghurt, perfect rice (see page 138) and the leftover lemon sliced into wedges for squeezing over.

EAT THE SEASONS

Spring vegetable noodle stir-fry

With toasted peanut sprinkle

You need

1 red onion

4 cloves of garlic

6cm piece of ginger

½ a bunch of coriander (15g)

1 red pepper

1 carrot

180g asparagus

100g baby courgettes
  or 1 small courgette

200g medium egg noodles
  (4 nests)

optional: ½ a red chilli

1 lime

75g unsalted peanuts

olive oil

100g sugar snap peas
  or mangetout

4 tablespoons low-salt soy sauce

1 Peel the onion and garlic and finely slice, then peel and matchstick the ginger. Pick the coriander leaves and finely chop the stalks.

2 Deseed and finely slice the pepper, and scrub and finely slice the carrot. Snap the woody ends off the asparagus and slice into 3cm pieces with the baby courgettes (or slice if using a regular courgette).

3 Cook the noodles according to the packet instructions, then drain and refresh in cold water (this stops them over-cooking).

4 Trim, deseed and finely chop the chilli (if using), and halve the lime.

5 Place a large non-stick frying pan (or wok) on a medium heat, add the peanuts and toast until golden, then tip on to a board.

6 Place the pan back on a high heat, drizzle in 1 tablespoon of olive oil, then add the onion, garlic, ginger, chilli and coriander stalks and stir-fry for 2 minutes, or until lightly golden.

7 Add the pepper, carrot, asparagus and courgettes, fry for a further 3 minutes, then add the sugar snaps or mangetout and the noodles for 1 final minute. Squeeze over half the lime juice and add the soy, then toss everything together.

8 Divide between plates, sprinkle over the coriander leaves, then chop and scatter over the toasted nuts. Cut the remaining lime into wedges for squeezing over.

 I've used spring vegetables here, but feel free to swap in different veggies depending on the time of year, or what you have to use up.

New potato and pesto focaccia

With oozy mozzarella

You need

1 x 7g sachet of dried yeast

500g strong bread flour,
   plus extra for dusting

olive oil, for greasing

250g baby new potatoes

50g breadcrumbs

1 x 125g ball of
   mozzarella cheese

100g your favourite pesto
   (see page 130)

1   Mix the yeast into 300ml of lukewarm water and leave for a few minutes. Tip the flour into a large mixing bowl, add 1 level teaspoon of sea salt, then make a well in the middle. Pour in the yeast mixture, then use a fork to bring in the flour from the outside to form a dough.

2   Knead on a flour-dusted surface for 10 minutes, or until smooth and springy. Place in a lightly oiled bowl, then cover with a clean, damp tea towel and leave to prove in a warm place for 1 hour, or until doubled in size.

3   Scrub the potatoes, halving any larger ones, then place in a pan of boiling salted water on a medium heat for 12 minutes, or until tender. Drain and leave to cool in a colander.

4   Lightly oil a 25cm x 30cm roasting tray, then scatter in the breadcrumbs and shake around so they stick to the oil.

5   Knead and punch the dough, knocking all the air out of it, then stretch it out to fill the tray. Use your fingers to gently push down and create lots of dips and wells.

6   Tip the potatoes into a mixing bowl and tear in the mozzarella, then add the pesto and toss together, breaking up some of the potatoes as you go. Spread the topping mixture evenly over the dough, drizzle with 2 tablespoons of olive oil, then press the topping down into the dips and wells, seasoning from a height with salt and black pepper.

7   Cover the tray with a clean damp tea towel, then leave to prove in a warm place for 1 hour, or until doubled in size.

8   Preheat the oven to 220°C. Very carefully – to keep the air in the dough – transfer the tray to the bottom of the oven and bake for 25 to 30 minutes, or until golden and cooked through.

Summery salmon traybake

New potatoes, tomatoes, beans, peas and pesto

You need

200g green beans

400g baby new potatoes

200g cherry tomatoes

200g frozen peas

olive oil

4 x 120g salmon fillets, skin on, scaled, pin-boned

½ a bunch of basil (15g)

4 tablespoons your favourite pesto (see page 130)

1 lemon

1   Preheat the oven to 200°C. Trim the green beans and scrub the potatoes, halving any larger ones.

2   Cook the potatoes in a pan of boiling salted water over a high heat for 12 minutes, adding the green beans for the final 2 minutes, then drain and tip into a 25cm x 30cm roasting tray.

3   Halve the cherry tomatoes and scatter into the tray, along with the frozen peas. Drizzle over 1 tablespoon of olive oil and season with a pinch of sea salt and black pepper, then toss together, and shake into a nice even layer.

4   Arrange the salmon fillets on top, skin side up, and roast for 15 minutes, or until the salmon is just cooked through and the skin is crispy.

5   Divide between serving plates, drizzling over any juices from the bottom of the tray, then pick over the basil leaves. Finish with dollops of pesto, and cut the lemon into wedges for squeezing over.

66 This is one of my favourite ways to enjoy salmon – chuck it together and get it in the oven. 99

Barbecued chicken lollipops

With pepper and pineapple salsa, and lemony couscous

You need

150g wholewheat couscous

olive oil

2 lemons

2 x 120g skinless chicken breasts

4 sprigs of rosemary (tied together with a piece of string)

1 teaspoon runny honey

1 red pepper

¼ of a small red onion

150g pineapple

optional: ½ a bunch of soft herbs, such as mint, flat-leaf parsley (15g)

4 tablespoons natural yoghurt

1   Soak 6 wooden skewers in cold water to stop them burning later on.

2   Place the couscous in a bowl with ½ a tablespoon of olive oil. Finely grate in the zest of ½ a lemon and squeeze in the juice, throwing the squeezed half into the bowl. Just cover the couscous with boiling water, then cover and leave aside to fluff up.

3   Carefully push 3 skewers horizontally into each chicken breast (trim the skewers, if needed), season with black pepper, squeeze over the juice of ½ a lemon and drizzle with ½ a tablespoon of olive oil.

4   You can cook the skewers on a hot barbecue or in a non-stick frying pan on the hob. Either way, cook them for 8 to 10 minutes, or until the chicken is golden and cooked through, turning regularly. For the final minute of cooking, use the rosemary sprigs to brush the honey over the chicken, giving it a lovely sticky glaze.

5   Halve, deseed and finely chop the pepper, then peel and finely chop the onion and pineapple, and scrape everything into a bowl. Add a squeeze of lemon juice and a drizzle of olive oil, then taste and season with sea salt and pepper, if needed. Pick and finely chop the herbs (if using), then add to the bowl and toss together.

6   Fluff up the couscous with a fork, season to taste with salt and pepper, and divide between serving plates.

7   Slice the chicken between the skewers, making sure it's cooked through – if it's not, give it a little longer. Place 3 chicken lollipops on each plate, and divide up the salsa. Serve with yoghurt for dipping, and cut the remaining lemon into wedges for squeezing over.

Autumn veggie chilli

Sweet potatoes, peppers and aubergine

You need

500g sweet potatoes

2 mixed-colour peppers

1 aubergine

1 onion

2 cloves of garlic

1 bunch of coriander (30g)

olive oil

1 teaspoon chilli powder

1 teaspoon ground cinnamon

2 teaspoons ground cumin

1 x 400g tin of kidney beans

1 x 400g tin of chickpeas

2 x 400g tins of plum tomatoes

4–6 tablespoons natural yoghurt

1 Peel the sweet potatoes and deseed the peppers, then chop into bite-sized chunks, along with the aubergine.

2 Peel and roughly chop the onion and peel and finely chop the garlic, then pick the coriander leaves, finely chopping the stalks.

3 Drizzle 1 tablespoon of olive oil into a large non-stick casserole pan on a medium heat, then add all the chopped ingredients and cook for 15 minutes with the lid on (leaving a little gap), stirring occasionally.

4 Stir in the spices and cook for 2 minutes, then drain and add the beans and chickpeas. Scrunch in the tomatoes (or tip in and break up with a spoon as you go).

5 Bring to the boil, then cook for 30 minutes on a low heat, or until thickened slightly, adding splashes of water to loosen, if needed.

6 Stir in most of the coriander leaves, then taste and season with sea salt and black pepper, if needed. Scatter the rest of the coriander leaves over the top and serve with the yoghurt for dolloping over.

66 I love this with perfect rice (see page 138) or served up on a baked potato (see page 142), or you can spoon it into a wrap or dollop it over nachos (see page 124). Yum! 99

Smashed squash quesadilla

With avocado yoghurt and lime

You need

400g fresh or frozen squash

1 teaspoon sweet smoked paprika

6 spring onions

30g Cheddar cheese

2 wholemeal or seeded tortillas

½ a ripe avocado

2 heaped tablespoons
 natural yoghurt

½ a lime

1 If using fresh, peel the squash and chop into 2cm chunks (deseed first, if needed), then cook in the microwave on high (800W) for 7 minutes, or until tender. If using frozen, defrost the squash in the microwave for 5 minutes, then cook on high for a further 5 minutes, or until tender.

2 Mash the cooked squash with the sweet smoked paprika and a pinch of sea salt and black pepper.

3 Place a large non-stick frying pan on a medium heat to warm up while you trim and finely slice the spring onions and grate the Cheddar.

4 Sprinkle half the cheese and spring onions over one tortilla, and top with the mashed squash. Scatter over the rest of the spring onions and cheese, and top with the second tortilla, pressing down slightly.

5 Carefully transfer to the hot pan and cook for 3 minutes, then flip over and continue cooking for 1 to 2 further minutes, or until golden and crisp. Slide on to a board and cut into 8 wedges.

6 Mash the avocado (destone, if needed) with the yoghurt, and serve on the side for dunking. Slice the lime into wedges for squeezing over.

Winter chicken hotpot

With a cheat's sauce and chipolatas

You need

2 onions

2 carrots

4 chicken thighs, skin off, bone out

4 chipolatas

olive oil

2 x 400g tins of chicken and
  mushroom soup

600g potatoes

1 teaspoon dried thyme

1   Peel and roughly chop the onions and carrots, and chop the chicken
    and chipolatas into 3cm chunks.

2   Drizzle 1 tablespoon of olive oil into a 26cm round casserole pan,
    add the chopped vegetables, chicken and chipolatas and cook for
    15 minutes, or until lightly golden.

3   Tip in the soup and mix well, then simmer on a low heat for 10 minutes,
    or until thickened slightly.

4   Preheat the oven to 180°C. Scrub and slice the potatoes so they're
    just under ½cm thick (or rattle them through the thick slicer attachment
    of a food processor to speed things up).

5   Toss the sliced potatoes with a pinch of sea salt and black pepper, 1
    tablespoon of olive oil and the thyme. Carefully layer the potatoes
    over the stew so it's completely covered, overlapping them slightly.

6   Bake for 40 minutes, or until the potatoes are golden and tender.
    Delicious served with green beans, broccoli or peas.

" I love this when I'm tired after playing
sports – it makes me feel good. **"**

Steak sarnie

With crunchy winter slaw

You need

1 x 225g sirloin steak, trimmed of fat and sinew

olive oil

1 sprig of rosemary

2 small ciabatta rolls

unsalted butter, for spreading

creamed horseradish, mustard, tomato ketchup or brown sauce, to serve

Winter slaw

1 carrot

1 small parsnip

½ a small red onion

150g white cabbage

1 small eating apple

½ a lemon

75g natural yoghurt

1 tablespoon wholegrain mustard

1 Season the steak with a pinch of sea salt and black pepper and drizzle with 1 tablespoon of olive oil, then rub all over. Strip off and finely chop the rosemary leaves, then pat them on to the steak.

2 For the slaw, scrub and coarsely grate the carrot and parsnip, and peel and very finely slice the onion, then scrape into a mixing bowl

3 Remove any tatty outer leaves from the cabbage, then very finely slice into thin strips and add to the bowl.

4 Coarsely grate the apple, discarding the stalk and seeds, then add to the bowl. Finely grate in the lemon zest and squeeze in the juice, then add the yoghurt and mustard, and mix well.

5 Put a non-stick frying pan on a high heat. Once hot, carefully place the steak in the pan and cook for 2 minutes on each side for medium-rare, or until cooked to your liking, then remove to a board to rest.

6 Halve the ciabatta rolls – you can leave them as is or toast them alongside the steak in the pan. Lightly butter the ciabatta, then spread over the condiment of your choice.

7 Drizzle the steak lightly with olive oil and slice into strips, then toss in the resting juices and divide between the bottoms of the ciabatta.

8 Wipe the tops of the ciabatta through the remaining resting juices, sandwich together and cut in half. Serve with the slaw on the side, or stuff some into the sandwich, if you prefer.

Spicy tomato pasta

With homemade tagliatelle

You need

1 clove of garlic

olive oil

½ a red chilli

2 large ripe tomatoes

1 x pasta dough (see below), 125g fresh pasta or 75g dried pasta

Pasta dough (optional)

100g plain flour or Tipo 00 flour, plus extra for dusting

1 large egg

1   Peel and finely slice the garlic, then place in a saucepan on a medium heat with 1 tablespoon of olive oil and cook for 1 minute, or until starting to turn golden.

2   Deseed and finely chop the chilli, roughly chop the tomatoes, and add both to the pan with a splash of water. Cook for 10 minutes, or until the tomatoes have broken down into a chunky sauce, stirring regularly. Season to taste with sea salt and black pepper.

3   Cook the pasta in a pan of boiling salted water for 2 to 3 minutes if making your own pasta dough, or according to the packet instructions, then drain, reserving a mugful of starchy cooking water. Carefully toss the pasta with the sauce, loosening with a splash of pasta water, if needed. Delicious served with a fine grating of Parmesan.

To make fresh pasta dough

1   For the pasta dough, tip the flour into a mixing bowl and make a well in the middle. Crack in the egg, then use a fork to beat the egg until smooth. Gradually bring in the flour from the outside, adding a splash of water, if needed. When the dough starts to come together, dust your hands with flour and pat it into a ball.

2   Knead on a flour-dusted surface for 4 to 5 minutes, or until smooth and elastic (tweak with a splash more water or flour if you need to). Cover and leave to relax for 30 minutes.

3   Dust a clean work surface with flour, then use a rolling pin to roll out the pasta as thin as you can (aim for about 2mm), dusting it well with flour as you go.

4   Loosely roll up the pasta sheet, then use a sharp knife to slice it just over ½cm wide, tossing it with your fingertips to separate the strands.

Scruffy lasagne bake

Made with Buddy's Bolognese

You need

1 x Buddy's Bolognese
(see page 48)

200g frozen chopped spinach
(roughly 6 blocks)

250g fresh lasagne sheets

150g cottage cheese

100g Cheddar cheese

1   Preheat the oven to 200°C. Make the Bolognese or, if already made, warm it through in a large shallow casserole pan, with a good splash of water to loosen, then remove from the heat.

2   Add the blocks of frozen spinach to the pan of Bolognese, then tear in the pasta sheets and mix up really well to coat and separate, pulling some of the pasta sheets to the surface to create a top layer (hiding the frozen spinach underneath).

3   Spoon over bombs of cottage cheese, then grate over the Cheddar.

4   Bake for 25 minutes, or until golden and bubbling. Delicious served with a green salad.

66 Making a delicious lasagne feels quite grown-up, but this one is really easy. 99

Greens pasta

With crispy garlicky breadcrumbs

You need

100g garlic bread

1 head of broccoli

1 bunch of spring onions

3 cloves of garlic

olive oil

150g frozen peas

100g frozen spinach

300g dried farfalle

50g Parmesan or Cheddar
cheese, plus extra to serve

1 Whiz the garlic bread in a food processor or blender until you have fine crumbs, then toast in a large shallow non-stick casserole pan on a medium heat until lightly golden and crisp, and tip into a small bowl.

2 Break the broccoli into bite-sized florets, finely slicing the stalk. Trim and slice the spring onions, and peel and finely chop the garlic.

3 Drizzle 1 tablespoon of olive oil into the casserole pan and place back on a medium heat. Add the broccoli stalks, spring onions and garlic, followed 2 minutes later by half the peas and all the spinach.

4 Season with a pinch of sea salt and black pepper, then cook for 10 minutes, or until soft and the spinach has defrosted, stirring regularly.

5 Meanwhile, cook the pasta in a large pan of boiling salted water according to the packet instructions, adding the broccoli florets and remaining peas for the last 3 minutes. Finely grate the cheese.

6 Scoop 250ml of the starchy cooking water from the pasta pan and stir it into the vegetable pan with the cheese, then blitz until smooth.

7 Drain the pasta, broccoli and peas, toss with the sauce, and serve up, finishing with a fine grating of cheese. Serve the garlicky breadcrumbs alongside, for sprinkling over.

Easy meatballs and spaghetti

With bonus grated vegetables

You need

1 onion

4 cloves of garlic

1 courgette

6 chestnut mushrooms

olive oil

200g lean minced beef

200g lean minced pork

50g wholemeal breadcrumbs

20g Parmesan cheese,
   plus extra to serve

1 large egg

1 x 690g jar of passata

450g dried spaghetti

66 Definitely one of my favourite things to make, and everyone seems to love it!. **99**

1 Peel the onion and 2 cloves of garlic, then coarsely grate on a box grater with the courgette and mushrooms. Scrape everything into a large non-stick frying pan on a medium heat with 1 tablespoon of olive oil and cook for 10 minutes, or until softened, stirring regularly.

2 Tip the cooked vegetables into a mixing bowl and leave to cool, then add the beef, pork and breadcrumbs. Finely grate in most of the Parmesan and crack in the egg, then season with black pepper.

3 Squish the mixture together to combine, then with wet hands, take tablespoons of the mixture and shape into 30 little balls. Pop them on to a tray as you go, then place in the fridge for 10 minutes to firm up.

4 Place a large non-stick frying pan on a medium heat with 1 tablespoon of olive oil, then add the meatballs and cook for 8 to 10 minutes, or until golden brown all over, turning regularly.

5 Peel and finely chop the leftover garlic cloves. Create a little space in the pan between the meatballs, add the garlic for 2 minutes, then pour in the passata and give the pan a gentle shake.

6 Simmer for 20 minutes, or until the meatballs are cooked through and the sauce is thickened slightly, stirring occasionally. Taste and season with sea salt and pepper, if needed.

7 With around 10 minutes to go, cook the pasta in a large pan of boiling salted water according to the packet instructions, then drain, reserving a mugful of starchy cooking water.

8 Tip the pasta into the meatball pan and gently toss together, loosening with a splash of pasta water, if needed. Divide between bowls, serving the meatballs on top, and finish with a grating of Parmesan.

Peasto pasta

With smashed chicken

You need

320g frozen peas

1 small clove of garlic

1 bunch of basil or mint (30g)

40g pine nuts

40g Parmesan or Cheddar cheese,
  plus extra for grating

extra virgin olive oil

1 lemon

500g fresh lasagne sheets

4 x 120g skinless chicken breasts

olive oil

Veggie swap-in

Replace the smashed chicken with a poached egg (see page 22) or fried egg (see page 24).

1 Place the peas in a microwave-proof bowl and microwave on high (800W) for 3 minutes, stirring halfway.

2 Peel the garlic and place in a pestle and mortar with a pinch of sea salt. Pick in most of the herb leaves and bash to a paste. Add the pine nuts, finely grate in the cheese and muddle in 2 tablespoons of extra virgin olive oil. Drain and add the peas to the herby mixture, then roughly bash it all up. Squeeze in the lemon juice and season to taste.

3 Use scissors (go for crinkle-cut scissors, if you have them) to cut the lasagne sheets into fun shapes, tearing up the offcuts, then put aside.

4 Place the chicken breasts between two sheets of greaseproof paper, then use a rolling pin or the base of a heavy pan to bash and flatten them out to around 1cm thick.

5 Place a large non-stick frying pan on a medium heat with 1 tablespoon of olive oil, fry the chicken for 3 minutes on each side, or until golden and cooked through, then remove to a plate to rest – you'll need to work in batches.

6 Cook the pasta in a large pan of boiling salted water for 2 to 3 minutes, or until tender, then drain, reserving a mugful of starchy cooking water. Carefully toss the pasta with the peasto, loosening with splashes of pasta water, if needed.

7 Plate up the pasta, slice the chicken and arrange on top, and finish with the leftover herbs and an extra grating of cheese, if you like.

Cauliflower macaroni cheese

Topped with crispy breadcrumbs

You need

optional: 3 rashers of smoked streaky bacon or 6 rashers of pancetta

3 cloves of garlic

olive oil

3 tablespoons plain flour

1.3 litres semi-skimmed milk

1 tablespoon Dijon or English mustard

1 head of cauliflower (800g)

450g dried macaroni

150g Cheddar cheese

2 thick slices of bread

1 sprig of rosemary

1 Preheat the oven to 190°C. Lay the bacon or pancetta (if using) in a 25cm x 30cm baking dish, roast for 10 minutes, then remove.

2 Peel and finely chop the garlic, then place in a large shallow casserole pan on a medium heat with 3 tablespoons of olive oil. Stir in the flour and very gradually pour in the milk, simmer for 5 minutes, or until thickened slightly, then stir in the mustard.

3 Click off and discard any tatty outer leaves from the cauliflower, then break the rest into bite-sized pieces (including the leaves, removing any super-tough stalks).

4 Cook the pasta in a large pan of boiling salted water for 7 minutes, add the cauliflower and cook for a further 5 minutes, then drain.

5 Grate most of the Cheddar into the white sauce and mix well, then stir in the cauliflower and pasta, breaking up the cauliflower slightly with a potato masher as you go.

6 Place the cooked bacon or pancetta (if using) in a food processor with 1 tablespoon of olive oil and the bread. Strip in the rosemary and blitz to coarse breadcrumbs.

7 Transfer the pasta mixture to the baking dish, grate over the rest of the cheese and scatter over the breadcrumbs. Bake for 25 minutes, or until golden and bubbling. Delicious served with a green salad.

Tuna pasta

With tomatoes, leeks, fresh chilli and basil

You need

1 leek

optional: ½ a red chilli

1 clove of garlic

olive oil

1 x 400g tin of plum tomatoes

1 x 80g tin of tuna in spring water

150g dried spaghetti

2 sprigs of basil

Parmesan cheese, to serve

1   Halve, wash and finely slice the white part of the leek (save the green leafy part for making stock or soup). Deseed and finely chop the chilli (if using), and peel and finely chop the garlic.

2   Place a large non-stick frying pan on a medium heat with ½ a tablespoon of olive oil, add the chopped vegetables and cook for 5 minutes, or until softened, stirring regularly.

3   Scrunch in the tomatoes (or tip in and break up with a spoon as you go). Quarter-fill the tin with water, swirl it around to pick up the last bits of tomato and pour it into the pan.

4   Drain and flake in the tuna, season with a pinch of sea salt and black pepper, then bring to the boil. Turn the heat down to low and leave to simmer while you cook your pasta, stirring occasionally.

5   Cook the pasta in a large pan of boiling salted water according to the packet instructions, then drain, reserving a mugful of the starchy cooking water. Carefully add the pasta to the sauce and stir well over the heat, loosening with a splash of pasta water, if needed.

6   Divide between serving bowls, then pick and tear over the basil leaves and finish with a good grating of Parmesan.

Portable pasta salad

Crunchy vegetables, fresh basil and feta

You need

300g dried penne or pasta shells

½ a cucumber

1 red pepper

400g ripe tomatoes

optional: 1 handful of olives

½ a bunch of basil (15g)

extra virgin olive oil

red wine vinegar

100g feta cheese

1 Cook the pasta in a large pan of boiling salted water according to the packet instructions.

2 Slice the cucumber in half lengthways, scoop out and discard the seeds, then slice in half again. Chop into small pieces and place in a mixing bowl.

3 Deseed the pepper and chop to roughly the same size as the cucumber. Coarsely grate the tomatoes, discarding any tough skin and excess seeds, then add to the bowl.

4 Destone and tear in the olives (if using), along with the basil leaves, then add 1 tablespoon of extra virgin olive oil and 1 teaspoon of red wine vinegar.

5 Drain the pasta and refresh under cold running water, then tip into the bowl and toss everything together well. Season to taste with sea salt and black pepper, and scatter over the feta, to serve.

AFTER-SCHOOL BITES

Flavoured popcorn

Pick your favourite flavour

You need

olive oil

1 small knob of unsalted butter

40g popcorn kernels

Flavour combos

10g finely grated Parmesan cheese and a few pinches of sweet smoked paprika

½ a teaspoon of yeast extract spread loosened with 1 teaspoon of boiling water

2 teaspoons maple syrup or runny honey and a few pinches of ground cinnamon or ¼ of a teaspoon of vanilla bean paste

1   Place the olive oil and butter in a non-stick saucepan over a high heat. Once melted, add the corn and stir well to coat.

2   Cover with a lid and leave for a few minutes – as the popcorn starts to pop, gently shake the pan to make sure all the kernels have popped, then remove from the heat (it's ready when the popping slows down to just a few seconds apart).

3   Leave to cool for a few seconds, then drizzle or sprinkle over your chosen flavour combo (see below) and toss together well.

Next-level flavour

You can also supercharge your popcorn with things like balsamic vinegar or Worcestershire sauce, but to make sure it gets distributed lightly and evenly you'll need to use a spritzer bottle. You can usually find these in chemists and supermarkets. Simply decant your chosen flavour into the bottle and spritz away, tossing the popcorn as you go for even coverage, then leave to dry. If choosing vinegar, just make sure you choose a thin one to help it spritz well. Have fun!

No-bake porridge bites

Dried fruit, seeds and maple syrup

You need

50g Medjool dates

200g jumbo porridge oats

20g mixed seeds

100g mixed dried fruit

1 orange

1 tablespoon maple syrup

1 tablespoon vegetable oil

optional: 30g quality milk, dark or
white chocolate, for drizzling

1   Destone the dates, if needed. Put the oats, seeds, mixed dried fruit
and dates into a food processor and blitz until nicely chopped.

2   Finely grate in the orange zest, then add the maple syrup, vegetable
oil and a squeeze of orange juice. Blitz again to a soft dough.

3   Roll or press the dough out between two sheets of greaseproof paper
to around 1.5cm thick. Use a small cookie cutter to stamp out shapes
(each bite should weigh around 40g). Re-form and re-roll the offcuts
and repeat until you've used up all the dough.

4   Sit a heatproof bowl on top of a pan of lightly simmering water, snap
in the chocolate (if using) and stir occasionally until melted, then
drizzle over the porridge bites and leave to set.

5   Pop in an airtight container – they'll keep happily for up to a week.

Houmous and vegetable dippers

Extra-crunchy carrots, radishes, peppers, celery and cauliflower

You need

8 baby carrots

8 radishes

2 mixed-colour peppers

4 celery sticks

¼ of a head of cauliflower (200g)

optional: red or white wine vinegar

1 x 400g tin of chickpeas

1 small clove of garlic

1 tablespoon tahini or
   peanut butter

extra virgin olive oil

1 lemon

1 Wash, trim and halve the carrots and radishes, deseed the peppers and slice into strips with the celery. Break the cauliflower into bite-sized florets, discarding any tough stalks.

2 This is optional, but if you want to get your vegetables extra-crunchy, pop them into a bowl of cold water with lots of ice, a pinch of sea salt and a swig of vinegar 15 minutes before you want to eat them.

3 Tip the chickpeas into a food processor (juices and all), and peel and add the garlic. Add the tahini or peanut butter and 1 tablespoon of extra virgin olive oil, along with a squeeze of lemon juice and a pinch of sea salt, then whiz until smooth, scraping down the sides of the processor bowl, if needed. Have a taste and add more lemon juice, if needed, then transfer to a serving bowl.

4 Drain the vegetables (if you've soaked them) and serve alongside the houmous for dipping.

" My super-quick flatbreads (see page 140) or some toasted pita breads are also great for dunking and scooping. "

Stuffed folded tortilla

Ham, cheese, tomato, plus your favourite condiment

You need

1 small tortilla

1 slice of smoked ham

30g firm mozzarella or
Cheddar cheese

1 handful of cherry tomatoes

1 teaspoon your favourite pesto
(see page 130), mustard or all-
rounder tomato sauce
(see page 132)

1 Place the tortilla flat on a clean work surface and make a cut from the centre point downwards to the bottom edge.

2 Tear the ham over one quarter and grate the cheese over another.

3 Slice the cherry tomatoes and arrange in another quarter, then spread the pesto, mustard or tomato sauce in the final quarter.

4 Fold up (see pages 116–117), then transfer to a non-stick pan on a medium heat and cook for 4 to 5 minutes, or until beautifully golden, turning halfway. Delicious served with a crunchy green salad.

Flavour switch-up

Make this veggie by simply swapping the ham for a handful of baby spinach or jarred peppers. And if you're after a sweet treat, sliced banana, chocolate spread, toasted chopped nuts and fresh berries make a cracking combination.

Banana bread

With cinnamon, honey and nuts

You need

125g unsalted butter (softened), plus extra for greasing

2 large eggs

4 ripe bananas

2 tablespoons runny honey

2 tablespoons unsweetened apple juice

250g self-raising flour

1 big pinch of ground cinnamon

optional: 50g unsalted nuts, such as walnuts, pecans, almonds, hazelnuts

1   Preheat the oven to 180°C, and lightly grease the bottom and sides of a 1-litre loaf tin.

2   Beat the butter in a mixing bowl until creamy. Crack in the eggs and beat them with the butter (if it looks lumpy, don't worry, it will fix itself).

3   Peel and mash in 3 of the bananas so you've got a mixture of smooth and chunky. Stir in the honey and apple juice, then fold in the flour and cinnamon – try not to over-mix.

4   Bash or roughly chop the nuts (if using), then fold them through. Spoon the mixture into the loaf tin, then peel and slice the remaining banana and poke into the top.

5   Bake for 40 to 50 minutes, or until golden and cooked through – if you poke a skewer into the middle, it should come out clean.

6   Allow the loaf to cool slightly, then carefully turn out on to a wire rack to cool completely. Serve in slices – scrumptious spread with butter, nut butter, honey, jam or chocolate spread.

Mini quiches

With cheese, vegetables and smoky bacon

You need

125g plain flour,
  plus extra for dusting

65g unsalted butter (cold)

1 small onion

1 clove of garlic

olive oil

1 handful of your favourite
  vegetables, such as baby
  spinach, mushrooms, broccoli,
  peppers, cherry tomatoes,
  courgettes, peas

optional: 1 rasher of smoked
  streaky bacon or 1 slice of
  smoked ham

1 large egg

100ml single cream

60g your favourite cheese,
  such as Cheddar, Stilton,
  feta, goat's cheese

1   Put the flour into a mixing bowl, cube and add the cold butter, then rub in with your fingers until the mixture resembles fine breadcrumbs.

2   Add 2 tablespoons of cold water and mix until you get a rough dough. Bring the dough into a ball with your hands, then wrap and rest in the fridge for at least 30 minutes.

3   Peel and finely chop the onion and garlic, then place in a large non-stick frying pan on a medium heat with 1 tablespoon of olive oil and cook for 5 minutes, or until soft, stirring regularly.

4   Prep your chosen vegetables – clean and slice the mushrooms, slice the broccoli into very small florets, deseed and finely slice the peppers, finely slice the cherry tomatoes, dice the courgettes.

5   Add the vegetables to the pan (there's no need to cook the tomatoes) and cook for 3 to 4 minutes, stirring occasionally and adding splashes of water, if needed. Finely chop and add the bacon or ham (if using), and season to perfection. Crack the egg into a jug, pour in the cream and beat with a fork, then grate in most of your chosen cheese.

6   Preheat the oven to 190°C. Dust a clean surface and a rolling pin with flour and roll out the pastry so it's around the thickness of a £1 coin.

7   Stamp out rounds of pastry using a 10cm pastry cutter and gently push them into the wells of a muffin tray (leftover pastry can be pushed back into a ball and re-rolled). Prick each base with a fork.

8   Pop paper cases inside each well, fill with baking beans or uncooked rice, and blind bake for 15 minutes, removing for the final 5 minutes.

9   Divide the vegetable mixture between the pastry cases, pour over the egg mixture and grate over the rest of the cheese. Bake for 15 minutes, or until golden and just set. Delicious served hot or cold.

Homemade beans on toast

With smoky paprika and grated cheese

You need

olive oil

160g frozen chopped mixed
  onion, carrot and celery

½ teaspoon sweet smoked paprika

1 x 400g tin of cannellini beans

1 x 400g tin of plum tomatoes

2–4 slices of bread

unsalted butter, for spreading

Parmesan or Cheddar cheese,
  to serve

1   Place a large non-stick frying pan on a medium heat with 1 tablespoon of olive oil, then add the frozen vegetables and cook for 5 minutes, or until softened, stirring occasionally.

2   Add the paprika and cook for 1 minute, then tip in the beans (juices and all). Scrunch in the tomatoes (or tip in and break up with a spoon as you go), then season with a pinch of sea salt and black pepper.

3   Cook for 5 minutes, or until thickened slightly, stirring regularly.

4   Toast the bread, then divide between plates and spread lightly with butter. Spoon over the beans, and finish with a fine grating of cheese.

Easy swap-ins

If you don't have frozen mixed onion, carrot and celery in your freezer, you can easily swap to fresh. Simply trim, peel and finely dice one small carrot, onion and celery stick – just make sure they're softened (about 10 minutes), before adding the paprika.

Movie night veggie nachos

Sweetcorn salsa, popped beans and dressed avo

You need

1 x 160g tin of sweetcorn

6 spring onions

1 long red pepper

3 ripe tomatoes

optional: 1 red chilli

optional: ½ a bunch
  of coriander (15g)

2 limes

olive oil

4 wholewheat tortillas

1 x 400g tin of black beans

1 ripe avocado

50g feta cheese

natural yoghurt or sour cream,
  to serve

optional: chilli sauce, to serve

1 Preheat the oven to 180°C, and place a large non-stick frying pan on a high heat to heat up.

2 Drain the sweetcorn and trim the spring onions. Put the whole pepper, tomatoes, spring onions and chilli (if using) into the dry pan for 10 minutes, or until soft and charred, turning occasionally. Transfer the pepper and chilli (if using) to a bowl, cover and leave for 5 minutes. Remove the tomatoes and spring onions to a board to cool.

3 Tip the sweetcorn into the pan and cook for 2 minutes, then place in a separate bowl. Once cool enough to handle, roughly chop the tomatoes and spring onions and add them to the charred sweetcorn.

4 Peel, deseed and roughly chop the pepper and chilli (if using), pick and chop a few coriander leaves (if using), then add it all to the bowl with the juice of ½ a lime, a splash of olive oil and a pinch of sea salt.

5 Pile up the tortillas and cut, through the stack, into eight triangles (so you end up with 32 in total), then arrange in a single layer over two baking trays. Bake for 15 minutes, or until golden, turning halfway.

6 Drain and rinse the beans, pat dry with kitchen paper, then tip into the frying pan over a medium heat and leave for 5 minutes, shaking occasionally – you want them to pop open. Peel and destone the avocado, slice into chunks, then squeeze over the juice of ½ a lime.

7 Arrange the tortilla chips on a serving plate, top with the popped beans, tomato and pepper salsa and the dressed avo. Crumble over the feta, pick over the leftover coriander leaves (if using) and dot over the yoghurt or sour cream and the chilli sauce (if using). Cut the remaining lime into wedges for squeezing over.

SKILLS
FOR LIFE

One-cup pancakes

Use a cup instead of weighing scales

You need

1 cup of self-raising flour

1 cup of milk

1 large egg

unsalted butter or olive oil,
    for frying

1   Tip a cup of flour into a large jug. Fill the same cup with milk and pour into the jug, then crack in the egg and whisk together well.

2   Place a large non-stick frying pan on a medium heat with a small knob of butter (or use olive oil), then, once melted, add large spoonfuls of batter to the pan – you'll need to cook your pancakes in batches.

3   Wait for little bubbles to form on the surface of the pancakes, about 1 to 2 minutes, then use a fish slice to flip them over and cook for another 1 to 2 minutes, until golden on the other side.

4   Carefully wipe out the pan with a ball of kitchen paper, then add another small knob of butter and cook the next batch. Serve the pancakes right away, with your favourite toppings.

Top toppings

- Sliced banana, yoghurt and runny honey

- Blueberries, yoghurt and orange zest

- Grated apple or pear and maple syrup

- Mango or tinned pineapple, yoghurt, desiccated coconut and lime

- Sliced strawberries and nut butter

- Roasted rhubarb, yoghurt and toasted nuts

- Crispy bacon, avocado and maple syrup or chilli sauce

Pesto, three ways

Big flavour for very little effort

Green

1 small clove of garlic

1 bunch of basil (30g)

40g pine nuts

40g Parmesan cheese

extra virgin olive oil

½ a lemon

1 Peel the garlic and place in a pestle and mortar with a pinch of sea salt.

2 Pick in the basil leaves and bash to a paste.

3 Bash in the pine nuts and finely grate in the Parmesan, then muddle in 2 tablespoons of extra virgin olive oil.

4 Squeeze in a little lemon juice, to taste, and season to perfection with salt and black pepper.

Unofficial green

1 small clove of garlic

30g baby spinach

40g shelled unsalted pistachios

40g feta cheese

extra virgin olive oil

½ a lemon

1 Peel the garlic and place in a pestle and mortar with a pinch of sea salt.

2 Gradually add the spinach leaves and bash to a paste.

3 Bash in the pistachios, then muddle in the feta and 2 tablespoons of extra virgin olive oil.

4 Squeeze in a little lemon juice, to taste, and season to perfection with salt and black pepper.

Red

1 small clove of garlic

75g sun-dried tomatoes in oil

40g blanched almonds

40g Parmesan cheese

1 Peel the garlic and place in a pestle and mortar with a pinch of sea salt.

2 Drain and add the sun-dried tomatoes, then add the almonds, and bash to a coarse paste.

3 Finely grate in the Parmesan, then muddle in 2 tablespoons of oil from the tomato jar, and add a splash of water to loosen, if needed.

4 Taste, and season to perfection with salt and black pepper.

All-rounder tomato sauce

A flexible base for so many meals

You need

320g mixed vegetables, such as onion, leek, celery, peppers, carrots, courgettes, squash

2 cloves of garlic

olive oil

2 x 400g tins of plum tomatoes

1 bunch of basil (30g)

1   Prep, peel and trim your chosen vegetables, as needed, then roughly chop or coarsely grate on a box grater (or rattle them through the grater attachment of a food processor to speed things up). Peel and finely slice the garlic.

2   Drizzle 2 tablespoons of olive oil into a large non-stick pan on a medium heat, add the garlic and fry for 1 minute, then scrape in the chopped vegetables and cook for 5 minutes, stirring occasionally.

3   Scrunch in the tomatoes (or tip in and break up with a spoon as you go). Quarter-fill the tins with water, swirl it around to pick up the last bits of tomato and pour it into the pan.

4   Simmer for 20 minutes, or until thickened slightly, tearing in the basil for the last few minutes.

5   Remove the pan from the heat and season with sea salt and black pepper – you can either serve the sauce chunky, or leave it to cool slightly, then blitz to your favourite consistency.

big-batch favourite

You can use this handy sauce straight away, cover and keep it in the fridge for up to 1 week, or divide between ziplock bags, label and freeze in portions for another day. It makes a great topping for pizzas (see page 32), is delicious tossed through pasta (see page 134) and is the perfect base for things like lasagne, chilli or even soups.

One-ingredient pasta

Simply made with flour and water

You need

300g plain or Tipo 00 flour,
plus extra for dusting

1 Tip the flour into a mixing bowl, then gradually mix in just enough warm water (roughly 150ml) to bring it together into a ball of dough – if it feels a bit sticky, add a little extra flour.

2 Knead on a flour-dusted surface for 3 minutes, or until smooth and shiny. See below for how to cut or shape your pasta.

3 Cook the pasta in boiling salted water for 2 to 3 minutes for tagliatelle or pappardelle, or 5 minutes for pici (leave slightly longer if you've allowed the pasta to dry), then drain and toss with your chosen sauce.

For tagliatelle and pappardelle

Dust a clean work surface with flour, then use a rolling pin to roll out the pasta dough as thin as you can (aim for 2mm), dusting it well with flour as you go – you might find it easier to work in batches. Loosely roll up the pasta sheet, then use a sharp knife to slice it just over ½cm wide for tagliatelle or just over 2cm wide for pappardelle, and toss it with your hands to separate the strands.

For pici (think fine green bean-shaped)

Simply tear off 2cm balls of dough, about 10g in weight, and roll them out into long thin sausage shapes on a clean surface. The beauty is that they're all different, so anyone can do it.

Eggcellent pasta

If you want to see my method for fresh pasta using an egg, which has a slightly richer flavour and softer texture, see page 86.

Perfect rice

Beautifully fluffy results every time

You need

300g basmati rice

1 Pour 600ml of boiling water into a saucepan, add a pinch of sea salt and place on a high heat.

2 Tip the rice into a sieve and rinse under cold running water until the water runs clear (this will stop the rice sticking together as it cooks).

3 Once boiling, carefully add the rice to the water, give it a quick stir, then cover and cook on a low heat for 12 minutes, or until tender.

4 Leave to sit for 2 minutes, then fluff up with a fork.

Bonus flavour

Once you've mastered this method, feel free to give it a flavour boost by adding extra ingredients to the water as the rice cooks – citrus zest, desiccated coconut, a stock cube, sun-dried tomato paste, flavoured tea bags, fresh herbs or spices (cinnamon sticks, cardamom pods and turmeric all work well). Or you could simply finish with a good squeeze of lemon juice and some chopped spring onions. Have a play around until you find your favourite combination.

Super-quick flatbreads

Made with three simple ingredients

You need

200g self-raising flour, plus extra for dusting

8 tablespoons natural or Greek yoghurt

unsalted butter, to serve

1. Tip the flour into a mixing bowl, add a pinch of sea salt, then make a well in the middle. Add the yoghurt, then gradually mix together until smooth, using your hands once the dough starts to come together.

2. Dust a clean work surface and your hands with flour, then split the dough into 4 pieces. Stretch or roll out each piece to about ½cm thick.

3. Put a large non-stick frying pan on a medium-high heat to warm up.

4. Once hot, carefully add the dough to the pan and cook for 2 to 3 minutes on each side, or until golden and puffed up – you may need to work in batches. Spread each lightly with butter, then serve.

> **❝** You can eat these flatbreads simply with honey or jam, you can top them with eggs (see pages 22–25) or serve them with my vegetable curry (see page 60). I sometimes like to mix crushed garlic with a little butter, then spread it over the warm flatbreads for an epic garlic bread. Seriously tasty! You can even roll the dough into little balls, if you're a big dough ball fan – the possibilities are endless! **❞**

Baked potatoes

Serve with your favourite toppings

You need

4 baking potatoes

olive oil

1   Preheat the oven to 190°C. Scrub the potatoes under cold running water, then pat dry.

2   Prick all over with a fork, then drizzle each potato with 1 teaspoon of olive oil, season lightly with sea salt and black pepper, then rub all over and place on a baking tray.

3   Bake for around 1 hour (depending on how big your potato is), or until golden and cooked through.

4   Cut the potato open straight away – this will stop the inside steaming and becoming soggy.

Top toppings

- A knob of butter and your favourite grated cheese

- Homemade beans (see page 122) and grated Cheddar

- Tinned tuna, sweetcorn and mayonnaise

- Shake, rattle and roll rainbow salad (see page 144)

- Buddy's Bolognese (see page 48) and finely grated Parmesan

- Autumn veggie chilli (see page 74), sour cream and diced avocado

- Vegetable curry with cooling cucumber yoghurt (see page 60)

- Sausage and bean casserole (see page 54)

Shake, rattle and roll rainbow salad

With jam jar dressings

You need

2 x quick jam jar dressings
(see page 146)

4 small raw beetroot, different
colours if possible
(roughly 150g)

2 large carrots

160g red cabbage

160g white cabbage

2 firm pears

1 bunch of soft herbs,
such as mint, chives, flat-leaf
parsley, tarragon (30g)

150g shelled walnuts or pecans

Fantastic leftovers

This salad is delicious rolled
up in a wrap with a grating
of cheese or shredded roast
chicken – great for a picnic
or packed lunch, just pack the
salad elements separately and
quickly assemble just before
tucking in.

1 Make your chosen jam jar dressings – you can stick with one type or
serve up a mixture.

2 Scrub the beetroot and carrots under cold running water, then trim
and halve them. Trim away the cabbage stalks, cut into quarters, then
core the pears and slice into quarters, discarding the stalks.

3 Put the coarse grater attachment into a food processor and push
through all the vegetables in the following order (so the red cabbage
and beets are at the bottom of the processor bowl and the juice
doesn't stain everything else): red cabbage, beets, carrots, white
cabbage and finally the pears, or use a box grater to do this by hand.

4 Turn the contents of the bowl out on to a large serving platter so you
get piles of rainbow colours.

5 Pick and finely chop the herb leaves and place in a small bowl, then
crumble the nuts (bash first, if easier) into another small bowl.

6 Serve the platter, herbs, nuts and dressings in the middle of the table
so that everyone can make and dress their own salad – just remember
you can always add more dressing but you can't take it away.

Quick jam jar dressings

Lemon, yoghurt or strawberry and balsamic

Lemon

1 lemon

6 tablespoons extra virgin olive oil

1 tablespoon runny honey

1   Squeeze the lemon juice into a jam jar, add the extra virgin olive oil and the honey, then season with a pinch of sea salt and black pepper.

2   Put the lid on the jar and shake well.

Yoghurt

5 tablespoons natural yoghurt

2 tablespoons white or red wine vinegar

1 tablespoon extra virgin olive oil

1 sprig of flat-leaf parsley

1 sprig of mint

1   Put the yoghurt, vinegar and extra virgin olive oil into a jam jar.

2   Pick and finely chop the herb leaves, then add to the jar with a pinch of sea salt and black pepper.

3   Put the lid on the jar and shake well.

Strawberry and balsamic

6 ripe strawberries

6 tablespoons extra virgin olive oil

2 tablespoons balsamic vinegar

1   Coarsely grate the strawberries, then place in a jam jar.

2   Add the extra virgin olive oil and balsamic vinegar, then season with a pinch of sea salt and black pepper.

3   Put the lid on the jar and shake well.

SWEET
TREATS

Choccy microwave mug cake

With banana or raspberries

You need

100g dark chocolate (70%)

100g unsalted butter (cold)

2 tablespoons runny honey

2 bananas or 200g raspberries

2 medium eggs

70g self-raising flour

50g quality milk or white chocolate

optional: 6 tablespoons natural yoghurt

1 Snap the dark chocolate into a large mixing bowl. Cube and add the butter, then drizzle in the honey.

2 Microwave in 30-second blasts on a medium heat (600W), stirring after every time, until the chocolate has completely melted.

3 Peel and mash half the banana, or half the raspberries, and add to the chocolate mixture. Crack in the eggs, beat with a fork, then fold in the flour with a pinch of sea salt.

4 Divide the mixture between 6 small microwave-proof mugs or cups.

5 Break the milk or white chocolate into chunks and push them into the mixture, then microwave in two batches on high (800W) for 1½ minutes, or until risen and slightly gooey in the middle.

6 Slice the leftover banana and divide between the mugs, or simply dot over the raspberries, and serve with a dollop of yoghurt (if using).

66 Me and my sister Petal make these almost every week for a quick chocolately treat. 99

Ginger nut biscuits

With a touch of cinnamon

You need

100g self-raising flour

1 level teaspoon bicarbonate of soda

1½ teaspoons ground ginger

½ teaspoon ground cinnamon

50g golden caster sugar

50g unsalted butter

2 tablespoons golden syrup

1   Preheat the oven to 170°C and line two large baking trays with greaseproof paper.

2   Place the flour, bicarbonate of soda, ginger, cinnamon and sugar in a mixing bowl and mix well. Melt the butter with the syrup in a small pan, then pour into the bowl and mix to a soft dough.

3   Divide the dough into 16 portions and roll each piece into a ball Place on the lined trays, leaving a gap between them, then press down to flatten slightly.

4   Bake for 12 minutes, or until beautifully golden and starting to crack Leave to cool on the trays for 10 minutes, then transfer to a wire rack to cool completely.

Grilled fruit salad

Finished with lime and mint

You need

½ a pineapple

½ a cantaloupe melon

3 ripe kiwi fruit

200g strawberries

200g seedless grapes

1 lime

½ a bunch of mint (15g)

coconut or natural yoghurt,
   to serve

1   Soak 12 wooden skewers in cold water to stop them burning later on, and preheat your barbecue or griddle pan.

2   Peel and core the pineapple, peel and deseed the melon, then chop them both into 3cm chunks. Peel and quarter the kiwis, and trim the tops off the strawberries, halving any larger ones. Pick the grapes off the stalks. Gently thread the fruit on to the skewers.

3   Carefully transfer them to the barbecue or griddle pan and cook for 2 or 3 minutes on each side, then slide the fruit off the skewers into a serving bowl or on to a platter – you may need to work in batches.

4   Squeeze over the lime juice, tear over the mint leaves, and toss it all together. Serve with the yoghurt for dipping or dolloping over.

Helpful hack

If you're finding that some of your fruit is wobbly on the skewer, use the grapes to secure the ends, as they sit nice and tightly on the skewer.

Party tray cake

With fresh berries and sprinkles

You need

225g unsalted butter (softened), plus extra for greasing

225g golden caster sugar

4 large eggs

225g self-raising flour

1 heaped teaspoon baking powder

1 teaspoon vanilla bean paste

Buttercream and topping

150g unsalted butter (softened)

1 teaspoon vanilla bean paste

225g icing sugar

25g naturally coloured hundreds and thousands

1 Preheat the oven to 160°C, then lightly grease a 25cm x 30cm roasting tray and line it with a sheet of damp greaseproof paper.

2 In a food processor, blitz the butter and sugar together until light and fluffy (or you can do this by hand). One by one, crack in the eggs, then add the flour, baking powder and vanilla bean paste, and keep blitzing until smooth.

3 Spoon the mixture into the lined tray and spread out evenly. Bake for 25 minutes, or until golden and risen – if you poke a skewer into the middle, it should come out clean. Cool a little in the tin, then transfer to a wire rack to cool completely.

4 To make the buttercream, cut the butter into cubes, then beat with the vanilla bean paste for 2 minutes, or until creamy (save yourself a bit of time by using a free-standing mixer, if you have one).

5 Sift the icing sugar into a mixing bowl, then gradually add it to the butter, a few spoonfuls at a time. Once all the icing sugar has been incorporated, beat for a further 4 to 5 minutes, or until pale and fluffy.

6 Add 1 small splash of water to the buttercream and fold through to loosen slightly, if needed, then spread over the surface of the cake, using a spatula to smooth out and spread it right to the edges.

7 Sprinkle over the hundreds and thousands, then serve as is or decorate with things like berries, chocolate shavings and lots of candles. Enjoy!

Totally tropical pavlova

With passion fruit, kiwi, banana and coconut

You need

4 large eggs

200g caster sugar

1 lime

250g Greek yoghurt

4 ripe kiwi fruit

2 bananas

2 passion fruit

1 tablespoon desiccated coconut

optional: 1 sprig of mint

1   Preheat the oven to 130°C, and line a large baking tray with greaseproof paper.

2   Separate the eggs, placing the whites in a large clean mixing bowl (save the yolks for another recipe). Using a hand whisk or a free-standing mixer, beat the egg whites on the high-speed setting until they form firm peaks – you'll know the meringue is thick enough if you can tip the bowl upside down over your head and it doesn't fall out.

3   While still whisking, gradually add the caster sugar and a pinch of sea salt. Whisk for a further 4 to 5 minutes, or until white and glossy. Dip a clean finger into the mix and rub against your thumb – if the mixture feels grainy, keep whisking for a further 2 minutes.

4   Dot a tiny bit of meringue on each corner of the greaseproof, then turn it over and press down – this will secure it to the tray. Dollop the mixture on to the tray and spread it out into a 25cm round, using the back of a spoon to create little wispy bits on the top.

5   Bake for 1 hour 15 minutes, or until crisp on the outside and chewy in the middle, then turn the oven off and leave to cool in the oven.

6   When you're ready to assemble, finely grate the lime zest and mix with the yoghurt. Carefully peel and slice the kiwi fruit (a mixture of rounds and half-moon shapes looks nice), peel and slice the bananas, then squeeze over the lime juice and gently toss together.

7   Spoon the yoghurt on to the meringue and smooth it out. Arrange the kiwi and banana nicely on top, then cut the passion fruit in half and spoon over the flesh. Sprinkle over the desiccated coconut, then pick, chop and scatter over the mint (if using).

Quick fruity fro-yo

Yoghurt, lime and runny honey

You need

500g your favourite frozen fruit,
   such as raspberries, blueberries,
   blackberries, mango, banana

500g natural yoghurt

1 lime

optional: 2 sprigs of mint

runny honey, to taste

1   Place the frozen fruit (you can stick to one type, or choose your favourite combination) in a blender with the yoghurt.

2   Finely grate in the lime zest and squeeze in all the juice. Pick in the mint leaves (if using).

3   Blitz until smooth, then have a taste and sweeten with a little honey, if needed.

4   Spoon into bowls and serve straight away, or if you want to be able to scoop it and/or serve it in ice cream cones, pop it into the freezer for 2 hours before serving.

Helpful hack

If serving in bowls or tumblers, pop them into the freezer to get nice and cold before you start – this will stop the fro-yo melting too quickly.

Apple and berry crumble

With a nutty oaty topping

You need

4 eating apples

400g fresh or frozen berries

½ an orange

100g unsalted butter

150g plain flour

35g unsalted hazelnuts

35g rolled oats

75g demerara sugar

1   Preheat the oven to 180°C. Peel and core the apples, chop into 2.5cm chunks, then place in an 18cm x 25cm baking dish.

2   Scatter in the berries, finely grate over the orange zest and squeeze in the juice, then mix well.

3   Cube the butter, then place in a mixing bowl with the flour and rub together with your fingertips until you have fine breadcrumbs.

4   Bash or roughly chop the hazelnuts, then add to the bowl with the oats and sugar. Mix well, then sprinkle evenly over the fruit.

5   Bake for 45 minutes, or until golden and cooked through. Delicious served with custard, yoghurt or ice cream.

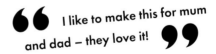

" I like to make this for mum and dad – they love it! "

Rocky road

With white chocolate drizzle

You need

olive oil, for greasing

100g dark chocolate (70%)

100g quality milk chocolate

125g unsalted butter

75g golden syrup

50g marshmallows

150g biscuits, such as ginger nuts
(see page 154), digestives

75g unsalted nuts, such as
pistachios, toasted hazelnuts

75g chocolate-covered
honeycomb

75g glacé cherries or dried fruit

50g quality white chocolate

1   Lightly oil a 25cm x 30cm roasting tray and line it with a sheet of damp greaseproof paper.

2   Sit a heatproof bowl on top of a pan of lightly simmering water, snap in the dark and milk chocolate, add the butter and golden syrup, and stir occasionally until melted.

3   Halve the marshmallows, snap up the biscuits, roughly chop or bash up the nuts, bash up the honeycomb and halve the cherries or dried fruit (if needed), then stir them into the chocolate mixture.

4   Pour into the lined tray and chill in the fridge for at least 4 hours, then carefully turn out.

5   Snap the white chocolate into a clean heatproof bowl and melt as described in step 2 (or melt in the microwave, if easier). Drizzle the melted chocolate over the rocky road, leave to set in the fridge, then slice up and serve.

Make it festive

Transfer the mixture to a 1-litre oiled and lined pudding basin before chilling, then turn it out, pour over melted white chocolate and decorate with artificial holly to turn it into a Christmas pud (see page 170).

Helpful kitchen notes

Choose good ingredients

Using good-quality ingredients in your cooking makes a big difference. When you're shopping, always have a look at what's available, pick and choose carefully, and if there are different levels of quality, buy the very best you can afford. When it comes to meat, fish, seafood and eggs, try to choose seasonally and responsibly, and look out for higher-welfare options.

Welcome seasonality

These days we can get almost everything all year round, but buying seasonally means that there are always new ingredients to look forward to. If you learn to shop for fruit and vegetables when they're in season, you will benefit hugely – it's not just about the nutritional and flavour benefits, it will often save you money, too.

Wash fruits and vegetables

Remember to give everything a good wash before you start cooking, especially if you're using it raw.

Handle food safely

Cooking food at the right temperature will ensure that any harmful bacteria is killed. When cooking burgers, sausages, chicken and pork, cut into the middle to check that it's no longer pink, that any juices run clear, and that it's piping hot. It's safe to serve steak pink in the middle as long as it's been properly sealed to kill any bacteria on the meat's surface. Once meat, chicken or fish are cooked, lift them out of the pan and serve them using clean utensils that haven't touched the raw food.

Organize your storecupboard

The store cupboard is an exciting place to be before you start to cook a recipe. It's a good idea to zone your spices, oils, vinegars, condiments and so on in separate areas to use the space efficiently. It's also a good idea to stock up on staples that have a long shelf life, such as rice, pasta, dried and tinned goods.

Freezing and defrosting

Remember to let food cool thoroughly before freezing, and get it into the freezer within 2 hours. Make sure everything is well wrapped, and labelled for future reference. Thaw in the fridge before use, and use within 48 hours. If you've frozen cooked food, don't freeze it again after reheating or defrosting it.

Manage your fridge

Being smart about how your organize your fridge will make it easier for you not to waste food. Keep any vegetables in the salad drawer so that they stay nice and fresh. Make sure any cooked food or leftovers are covered, and any uncooked meat and fish are well wrapped up and put on the bottom shelf to stop them contaminating anything on the other shelves. Put any food that's ready to eat, whether it's cooked or doesn't need to be cooked, on a higher shelf, away from the raw meat or fish. It's also a good idea to rotate newer and older food so that you use them in the right order.

A bit about oven temperatures

All recipes are tested in fan ovens – find conversions for conventional ovens, °F, and gas online.

Useful kitchen kit

Here's a list of basic kitchen equipment that'll help you make the recipes in this book, and beyond! Please don't worry if you don't have everything – just use what you've got available.

- ☐ Chopping boards
- ☐ Knives
- ☐ Weighing scales
- ☐ Measuring jug
- ☐ Measuring spoons
- ☐ Mixing bowls
- ☐ Speed peeler
- ☐ Box grater
- ☐ Fine grater
- ☐ Rolling pin
- ☐ Whisk
- ☐ Wooden spoon
- ☐ Slotted spoon
- ☐ Rubber spatula
- ☐ Fish slice
- ☐ Tongs
- ☐ Colander
- ☐ Sieve
- ☐ Potato masher

- ☐ Tin opener
- ☐ Kitchen paper
- ☐ Greaseproof paper
- ☐ Tin foil
- ☐ Saucepans
- ☐ Non-stick frying pans
- ☐ Casserole pan
- ☐ Roasting trays
- ☐ Baking trays
- ☐ Baking dishes
- ☐ 12-hole muffin tin
- ☐ 1-litre loaf tin

Nice to have

- ☐ Food processor
- ☐ Blender
- ☐ Toastie maker
- ☐ Stand mixer
- ☐ Pestle and mortar

Knife skills for kids

Having good knife skills can make you more efficient in the kitchen, but you must take care when using these tools so you don't get hurt. It's important to keep focused on what you're doing and remember, practice makes perfect!

Here are some handy techniques that you can use to help you on your journey to good knife skills.

How to hold a knife safely

Place your thumb and forefinger around the base of the blade in a pinching position, then wrap the remaining three fingers around the handle of the knife. Your index finger and thumb should be at opposites, on either side of the blade, with the remaining three fingers loosely curled around the handle.

The bridge

Use the bridge technique to cut ingredients into smaller, more manageable pieces.

Form a 'bridge' over the ingredient with your hand, making sure the arch is nice and high so there's plenty of room for the knife to fit underneath. Hold the item securely with your fingers on one side and your thumb on the other, then pick up the knife with the other hand and position the blade under the bridge. Cut into the ingredient, pressing the knife firmly into the middle and sliding it back towards you out of your bridge. Once you've halved the ingredient, place it flat-side down and cut into smaller pieces, if required.

The claw

Use the claw technique to slice ingredients into thinner strips.

Place the ingredient on the board, flat-side down. Make a 'claw' by curling your fingers closely together over the ingredient, tucking them under so you can't see your fingertips. Pick up the knife with your other hand – the flat side of the blade actually rests against the first knuckle of the claw, protecting the fingers. Keeping the tip of the knife on the board, slice through the ingredient, sliding the knife forwards as you cut and then back. Repeat, ensuring you have a good grip and keep your fingers together at all times.

The bridge

The claw

Rock chopping

This technique uses a rocking motion to chop, combined with the claw to keep your fingers safe.

Hold the knife firmly in one hand and place the tip of the knife on the board at an angle of roughly 45 degrees. With the other hand, make a 'claw' over the ingredient, tucking your fingertips out of the way. Using the curve of the knife, push down and forward in a rocking motion – the end of the knife doesn't leave the board. Move your claw back before making each slice. Practice makes perfect: don't go too fast! The side of the knife blade should rest against the first knuckle of the guiding hand, helping keep the blade perpendicular to the cutting board. To make your next slice, move your fingers back along the item, keeping your fingers together and keeping a firm grip on the top.

Cross chopping

Cross chopping is used to cut ingredients into much smaller pieces – for example, fresh herbs.

Hold the knife firmly in one hand, place the tip of the knife on the board at an angle of roughly 20 degrees. Keep the fingers of your other hand rigid on the top edge of the lower half of the blade. Keeping the tip of the knife on the board, raise and lower the handle of the knife, like a guillotine, so it chops whatever is under it. Gather back the ingredients into the middle and continue to cross chop until you have the size you want.

Safety checklist

✓ **Secure your chopping board**

✓ **Never wave a knife in the air**

✓ **Keep the handle clean for good grip**

✓ **Always chop ingredients flat-side down, where possible**

✓ **Slice small pieces off round ingredients to create a flat, stable surface**

✓ **Don't chop too quickly**

✓ **Clean your knife safely**

✓ **Keep your knife sharp**

✓ **Always hold a knife in your dominant hand**

✓ **Practice makes perfect!**

Rock chopping

Cross chopping

10 TIPS TO LIVE HEALTHILY AND HAPPILY

My Dad's Nutrition Team helped me to make sure that the recipes in this book are the right balance between nutritious everyday foods and things to be enjoyed occasionally. The recipes can be enjoyed by your whole family, so just dish up smaller portions if you're cooking for little brothers or sisters. They've also got some handy tips on a good approach to building positive eating habits that are easy to remember and will help you on the path to leading a healthier, happier life.

1. Always eat breakfast!

Kick-start your day in the right way with a nutritious, balanced brekkie so you can rebuild your energy levels after hours of being asleep.

Did you know? Studies have shown that young people who eat breakfast have better memory and concentration levels.

2. Balance and variety are key

Eat from all five food groups to get the wide range of nutrients your body needs. The picture of the Eat Well Guide (see page 180) is a really clear way to see the balance you should be aiming for. Try to eat a balance across the week and you'll be in a great place.

3. Eat the rainbow!

This is a fun one – eating all different colours of vegetables and fruits is important because they each hold different vitamins and minerals that all play a part in keeping us healthy.

Challenge: Try to eat at least five 80g portions (or 40–60g portions for younger children) of vegetables and fruit a day – you can choose from raw, frozen, tinned or cooked!

Did you know? Dried fruit (30g), fruit juice and smoothies (150ml), beans and pulses (80g) can each only count as one portion of our 5-a-day.

4. Upgrade your carbohydrates

Carbohydrates are things like bread, rice and pasta, and provide the main fuel for our bodies. When you can, try swapping to wholegrain and wholewheat varieties, like wholemeal bread and brown rice. They help us to feel fuller for longer, and provide more vitamins, minerals and fibre than white carbohydrates.

Eat well guide

It's all about balance

Fruit and vegetables

such as grapes, tomatoes, broccoli, cauliflower, carrots, apples, peppers

Starchy carbs

such as potatoes, bread, pasta, rice, cereals, oats, couscous, quinoa

such as olive oil, rapeseed oil

Oils and spreads

such as beans, eggs, fish, lentils, nuts, meat

Protein

such as milk, cheese, yoghurt

Dairy and alternatives

5. Mix up your proteins

You'll find protein in things like beans, fish, eggs, meat, nuts and tofu. Try to include different kinds of proteins in your meals. Think of protein as the building blocks of our bodies – it is used for growth and repair, and is important for healthy muscles and bones.

6. Include dairy

Add dairy foods, such as milk, cheese and yoghurt to your meals – they're packed full of important nutrients, especially calcium for strong bones and healthy teeth. Non-dairy alternatives, like plant-based drinks, should have key nutrients added to them (look out for calcium, iodine and vitamin B12 on the label to make sure).

7. Hero healthy fats

Unsaturated sources of fat, such as olive, vegetable and rapeseed oils, as well as nuts, seeds, avocado and rich oily fish are healthiest for us. They provide us with essential fatty acids and help us absorb vitamins and nutrients from foods.

8. Know your sugars

Sugar is found naturally in things like milk and dairy products (lactose) and whole fruits and vegetables (fructose) and that's OK. It's great to include these foods as part of a balanced diet. Free sugars, which are added to food and drinks, and those that are found in honey, syrups, smoothies and juices, are best enjoyed occasionally, not all the time.

9. Season to taste

Taste your food before you add salt, as you may not need to add any. And seasoning with herbs and spices can be equally, if not even more, delicious – give it a try! Although we do need a small amount of salt, having too much isn't healthy for us.

10. Stay hydrated

Drink plenty – it's an essential part of life! Water, skimmed and semi-skimmed milk, and sugar-free drinks count. Juices and smoothies also count, but only one small glass per day.

Challenge: Try to drink six to eight glasses per day.

THANK YOU

Thanks so much to everyone who has helped and supported me on this amazing project – it's been SO much fun, and I'm really proud of how it's turned out. Special thanks to Mum and Dad, and to Poppy, Daisy, Petal and River, as well as the Cooking Buddies gang. You're the best!

And big thanks to the rest of the team:

David Loftus
Paul Stuart
Richard Bowyer

Beth Stroud
Rebecca Verity

James Verity
Davina Mistry

Ginny Rolfe
Isla Murray
Holly Cowgill
Maddie Rix
Maggie Musmar

Jenny Rosborough
Rozzie Batchelar
Lucinda Cobb

Tamsyn Zietsman
Lydia Waller
Rosalind Godber
Ashleigh Bishop
Letitia Becher
Richard Herd

Kevin Styles
Louise Holland
Zoe Collins

Louise Moore
Ione Walder
Dan Hurst
Elizabeth Smith
Clare Parker
Tom Troughton
Ella Watkins
Juliette Butler
Lee Motley
Nick Lowndes

Christina Ellicott
Anjali Nathani
Joanna Whitehead
Stuart Anderson
Annie Lee
Jill Cole
Emma Horton
Catherine Hookway

Sean Moxhay
Samantha Beddoes
Anna Stickland
Mark Drake
Alice Binks
Gurvinder Singh
Anita Goundar
Josh Javed
Jon Padovani
Amanda Doig-Moore
Renzo Luzardo

Index

Recipes marked V are suitable for vegetarians; in some instances you'll need to swap in a vegetarian alternative to cheese such as Parmesan.

For more inspiration:

bbc.co.uk/food
bbc.co.uk/iplayer
jamieoliver.com
penguin.co.uk
youtube.com/cookingbuddies

Penguin Michael Joseph

UK | USA | CANADA | IRELAND | AUSTRALIA | INDIA | NEW ZEALAND | SOUTH AFRICA

Penguin Michael Joseph, Penguin Random House UK, One Embassy Gardens,
8 Viaduct Gardens, London SW11 7BW

penguin.co.uk
global.penguinrandomhouse.com

Penguin
Random House
UK

First published 2024

004

Copyright © Buddy Oliver, 2024

Recipe photography copyright © Jamie Oliver Enterprises Limited, 2024

BBC wordmark and BBC logo are trademarks of the British Broadcasting Corporation
and are used under licence. BBC logo © BBC 2021

The moral right of the author has been asserted

Recipe & portrait photography by David Loftus

Cover portrait & additional photography by Paul Stuart (pages 4, 9 & 191)

Design by Jamie Oliver Limited

Colour reproduction by Altaimage Ltd

Printed in Germany by Mohn Media

The authorized representative in the EEA is Penguin Random House Ireland,
Morrison Chambers, 32 Nassau Street, Dublin D02 YH68

A CIP catalogue record for this book is available from the British Library

ISBN: 978–0–241–69189–2

For our nutrition guidelines and further information visit: jamieoliver.com/nutrition

www.greenpenguin.co.uk